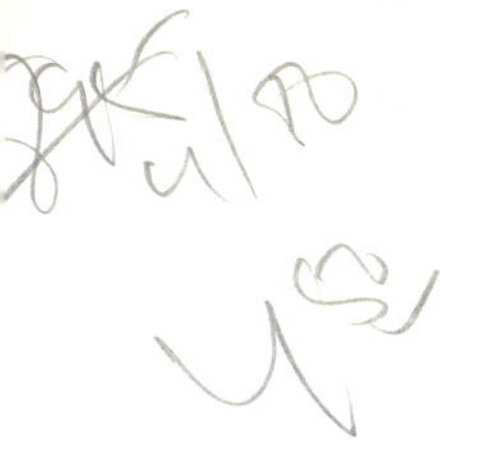

INNER GRACE

INNER GRACE

Photographs by
ABRAHAM MENASHE

ALFRED·A·KNOPF NEW YORK 1980

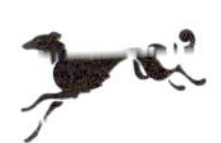

THIS IS A BORZOI BOOK
PUBLISHED BY ALFRED A. KNOPF, INC.

Published in the United States by Alfred A .Knopf, Inc., New York, and simultaneously in Canada by Random House of Canada Limited, Toronto. Distributed by Random House, Inc., New York.

Grateful acknowledgment is made to Random House, Inc. for permission to use the definition of grace in the Random House Dictionary of the English Language, Unabridged Edition.

Manufactured in the United States of America

First Edition

INTRODUCTION

The subject of *Inner Grace* is the multihandicapped institutionalized individual. This includes the retarded, the blind, and the cerebral-palsied.

Grace is defined as "elegance or beauty of form, manner, motion or act . . . the influence or spirit of God operating in man to regenerate or strengthen him." It is a state that exists in the joy of being as well as the effort of trying. The photographs embrace moments of innocence, accomplishment, serenity, pride, and struggle.

In accepting the limitations that life imposes on us, we can often overcome them. This is demonstrated by the youth in the pool who, despite a twisted spine and limited muscle movements, yields to the water, and in so doing learns how to swim.

The images reveal beauty in the distorted body and bring us closer to the conquering spirit in man. As we learn to carry our burdens well, in the yielding and in the striving, we become imbued with the favor and love of God. This assistance, the influence of the freely given, is grace.

To me the photographs form a prayer—not only in the making of them, but now in the sharing of them.

Abraham Menashe

INNER GRACE

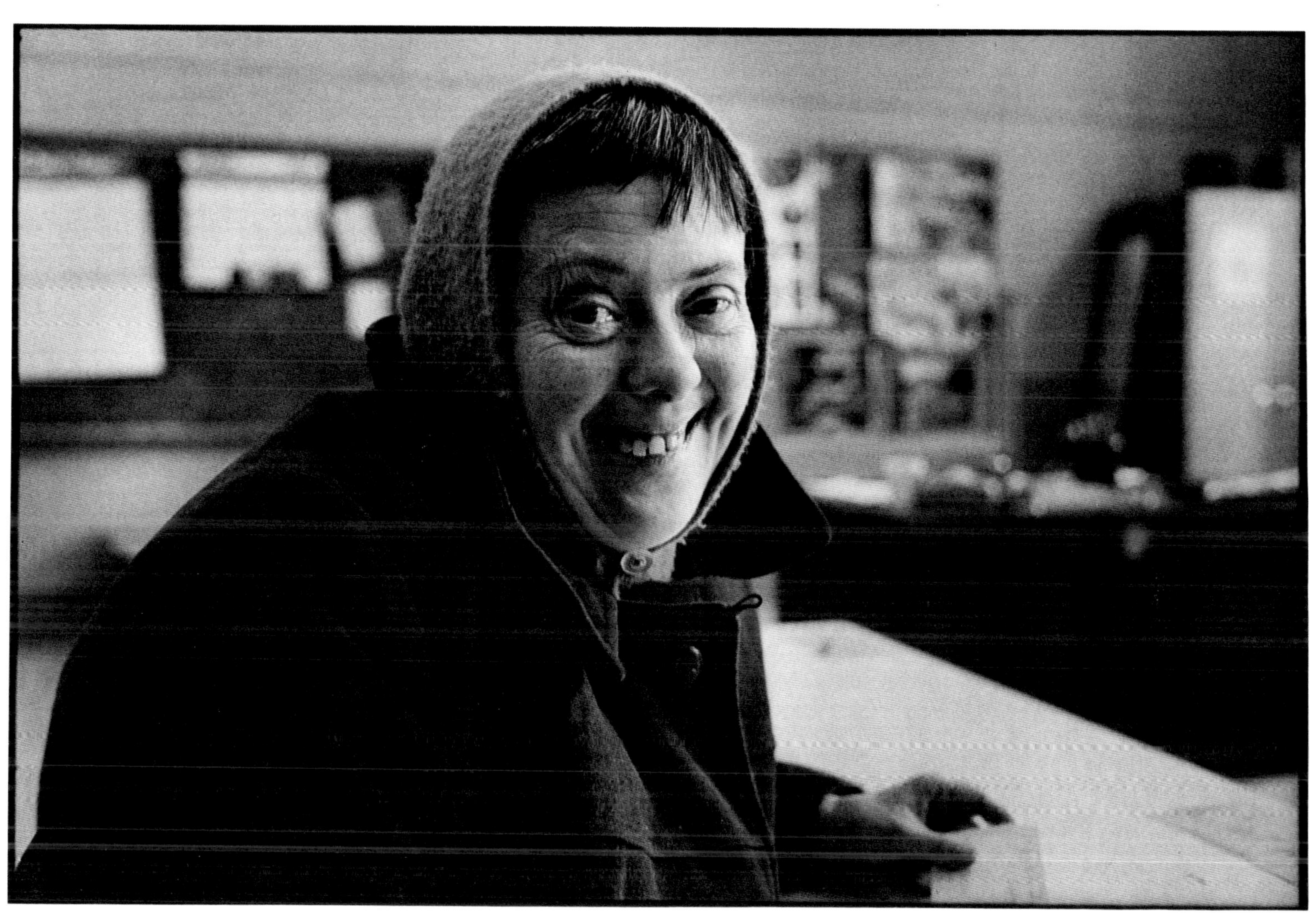

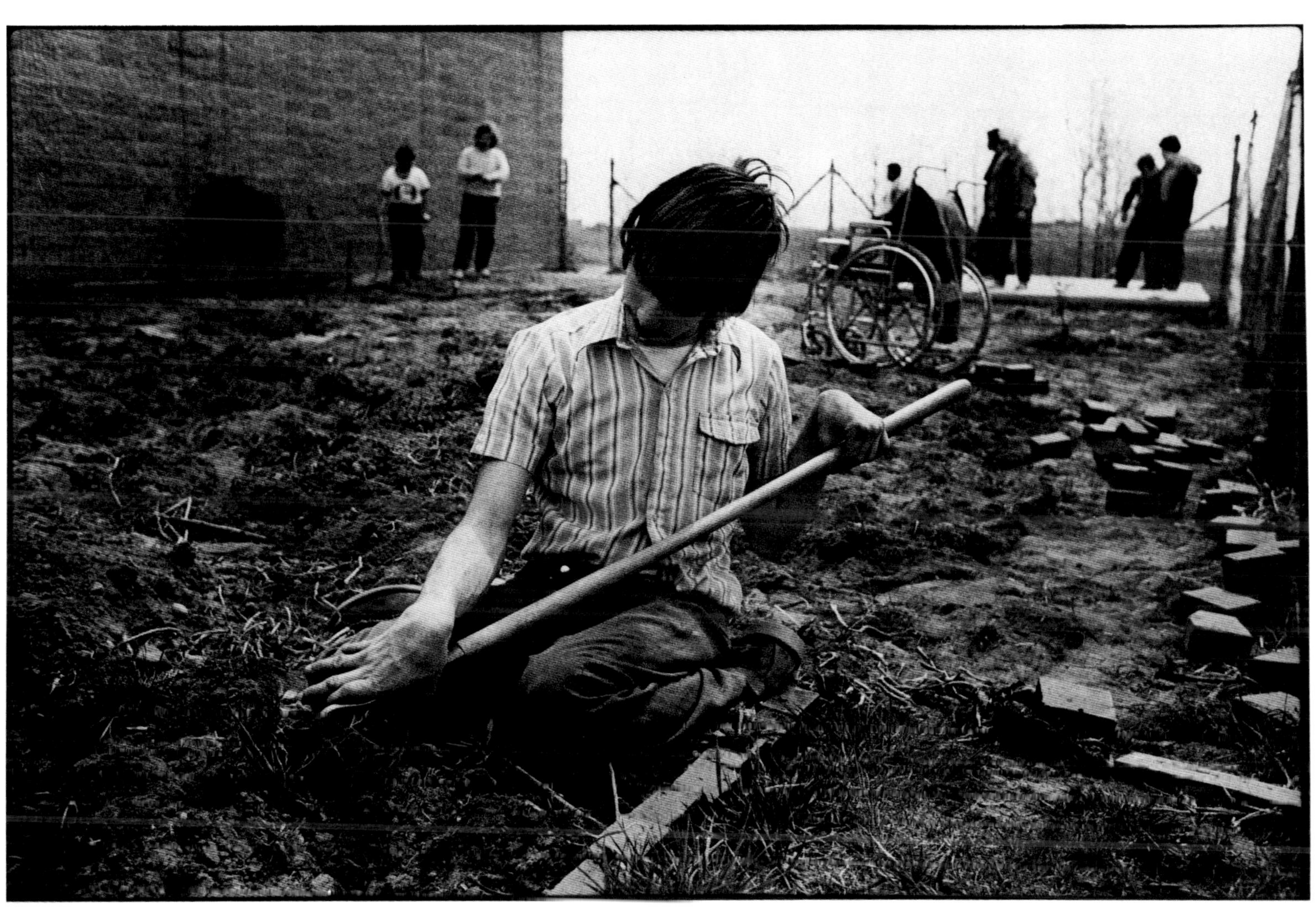

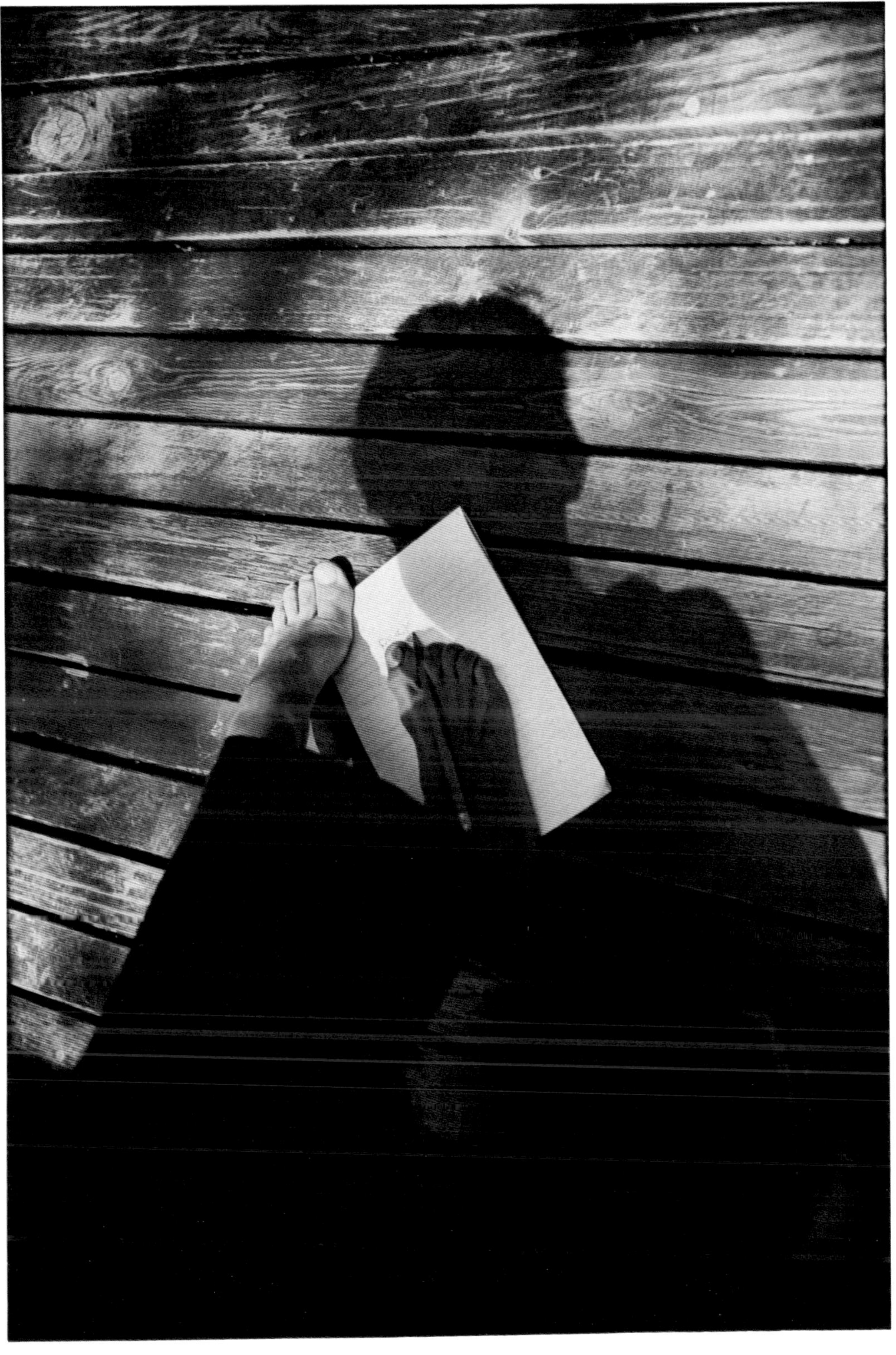

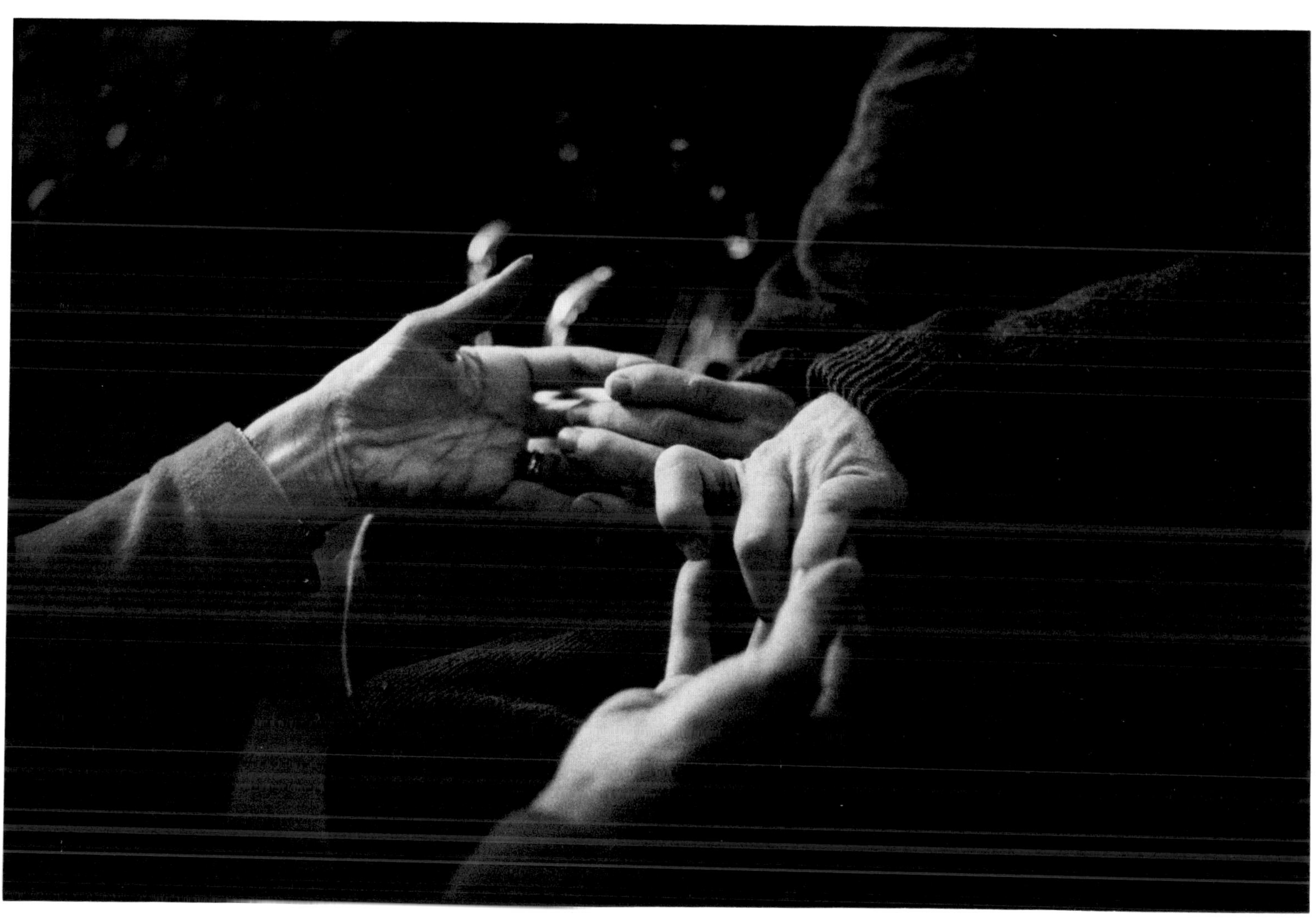

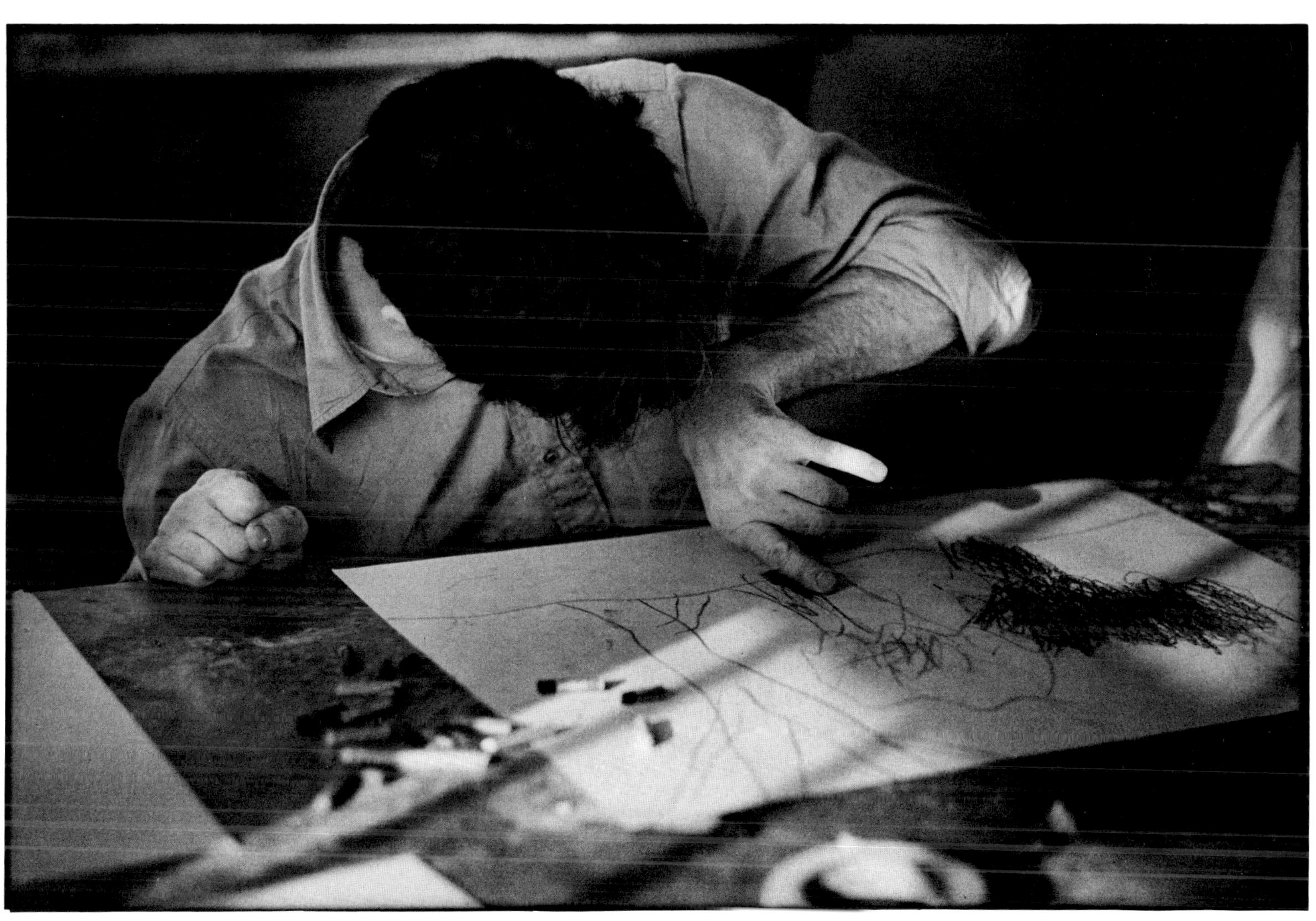

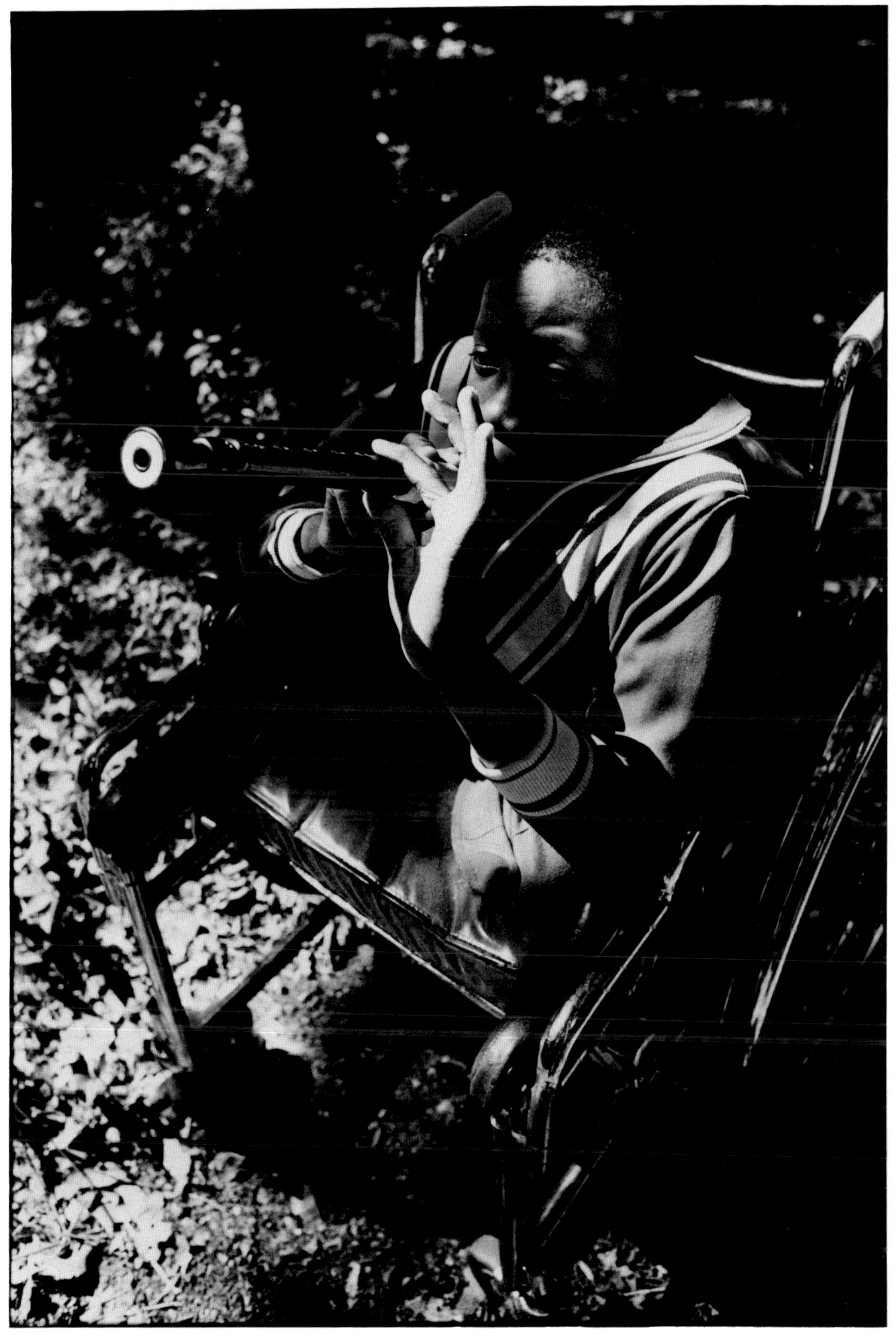

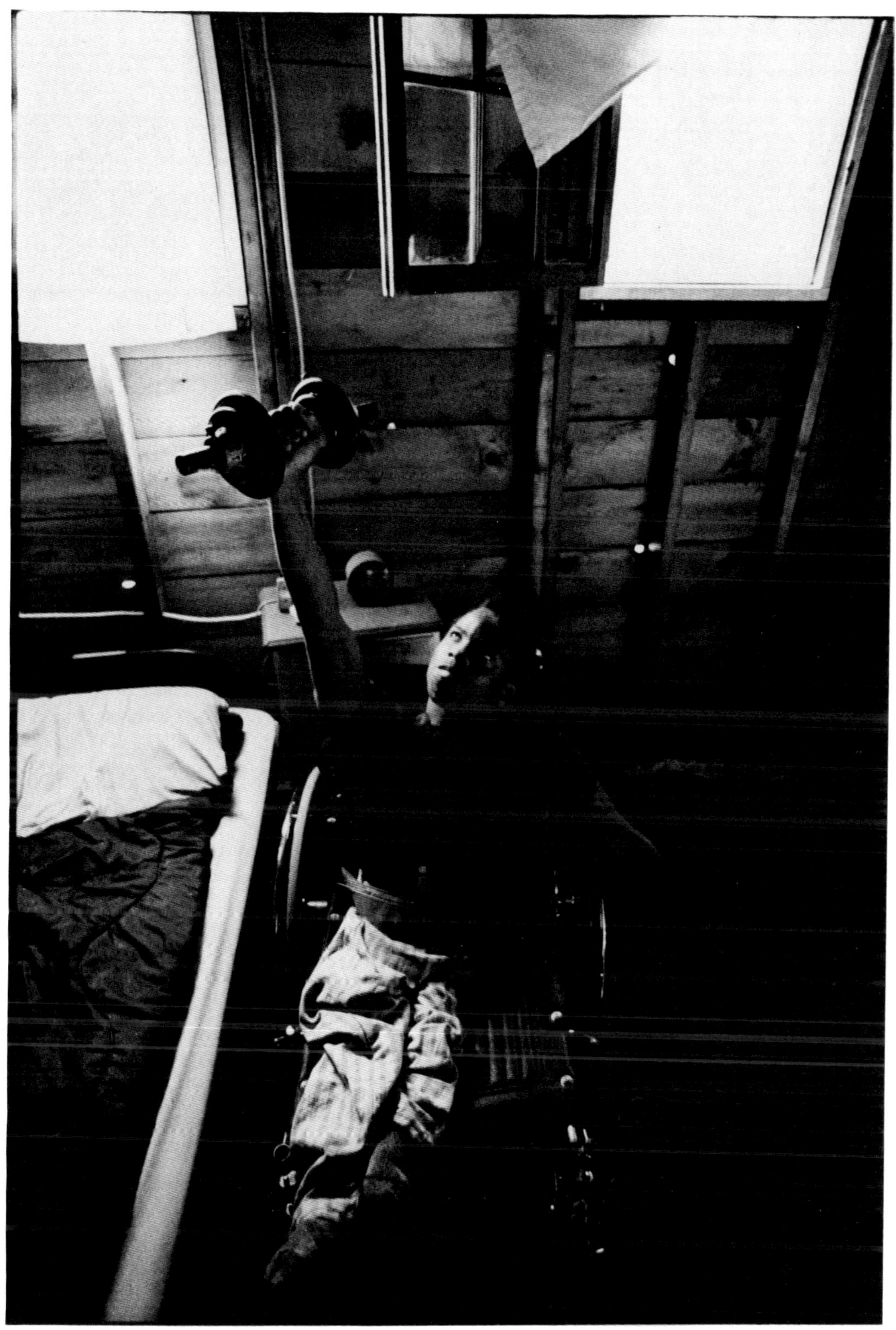

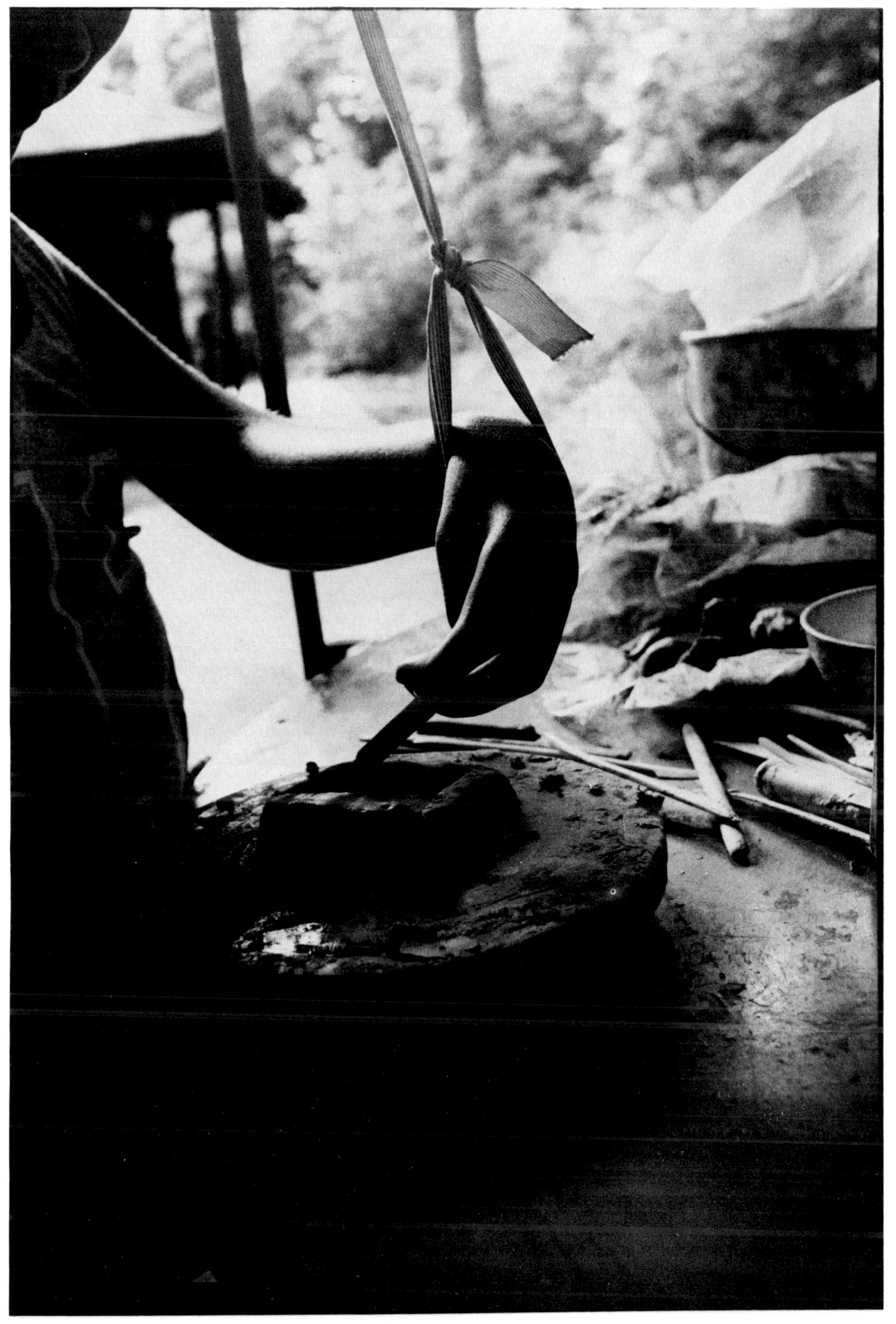

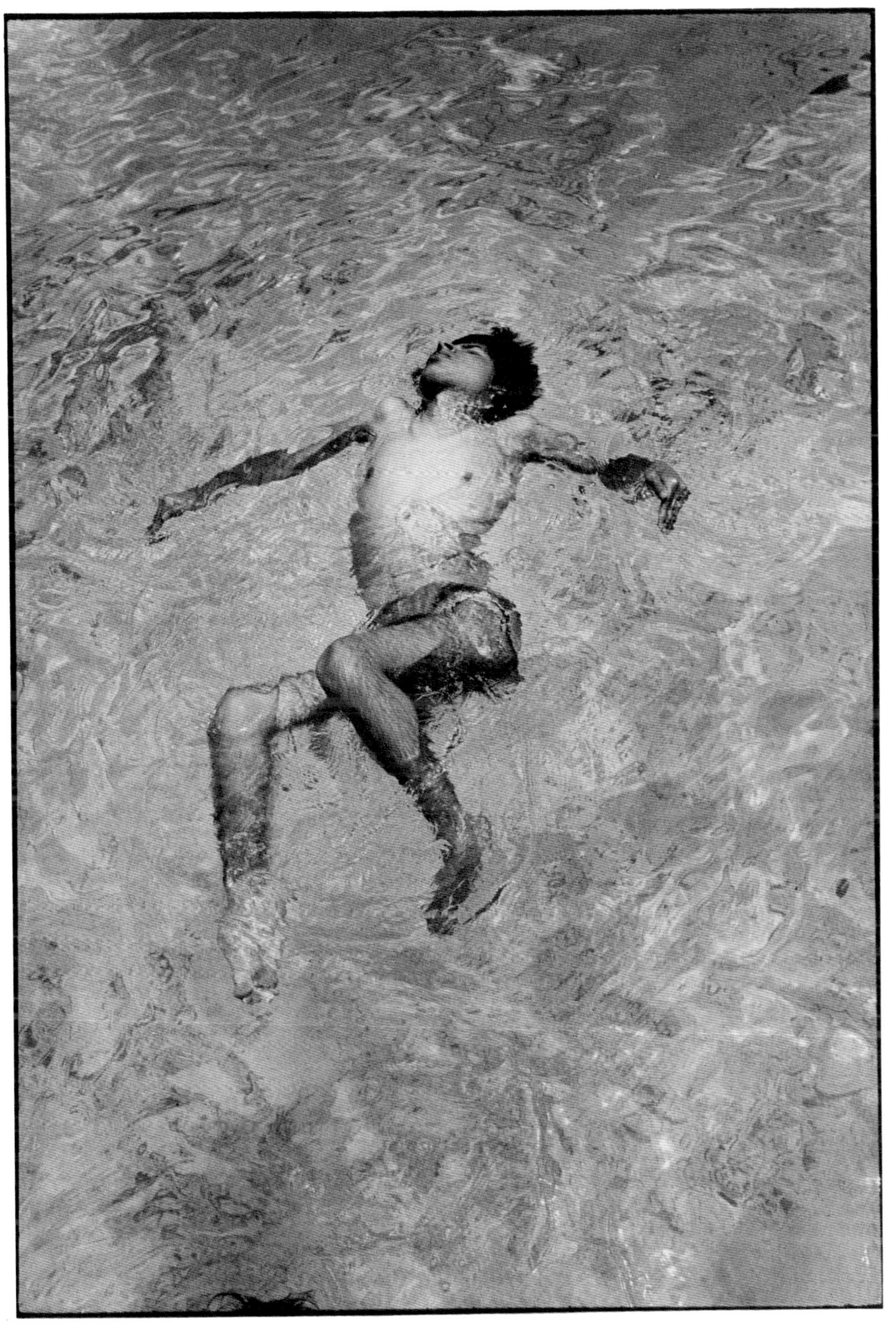

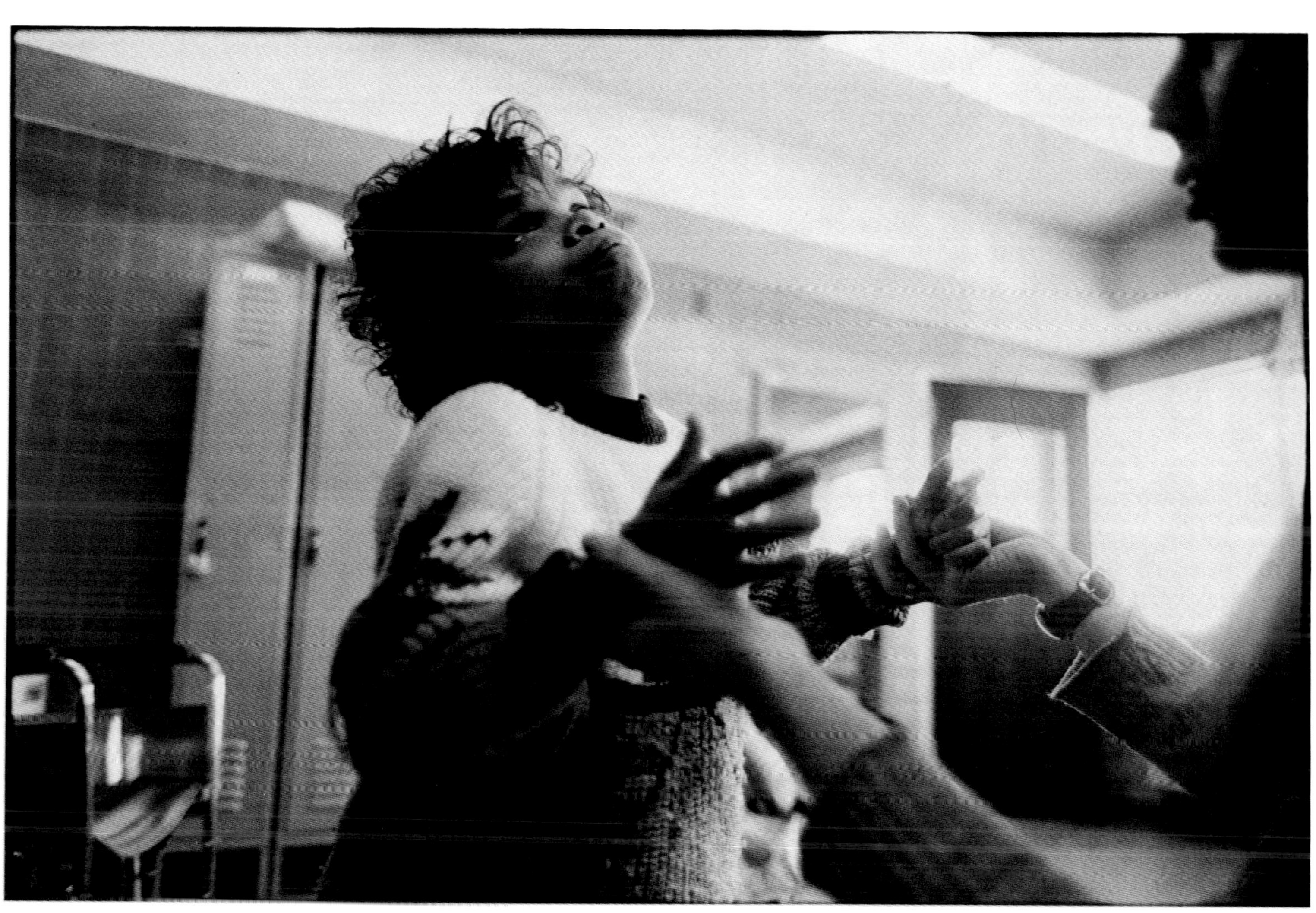

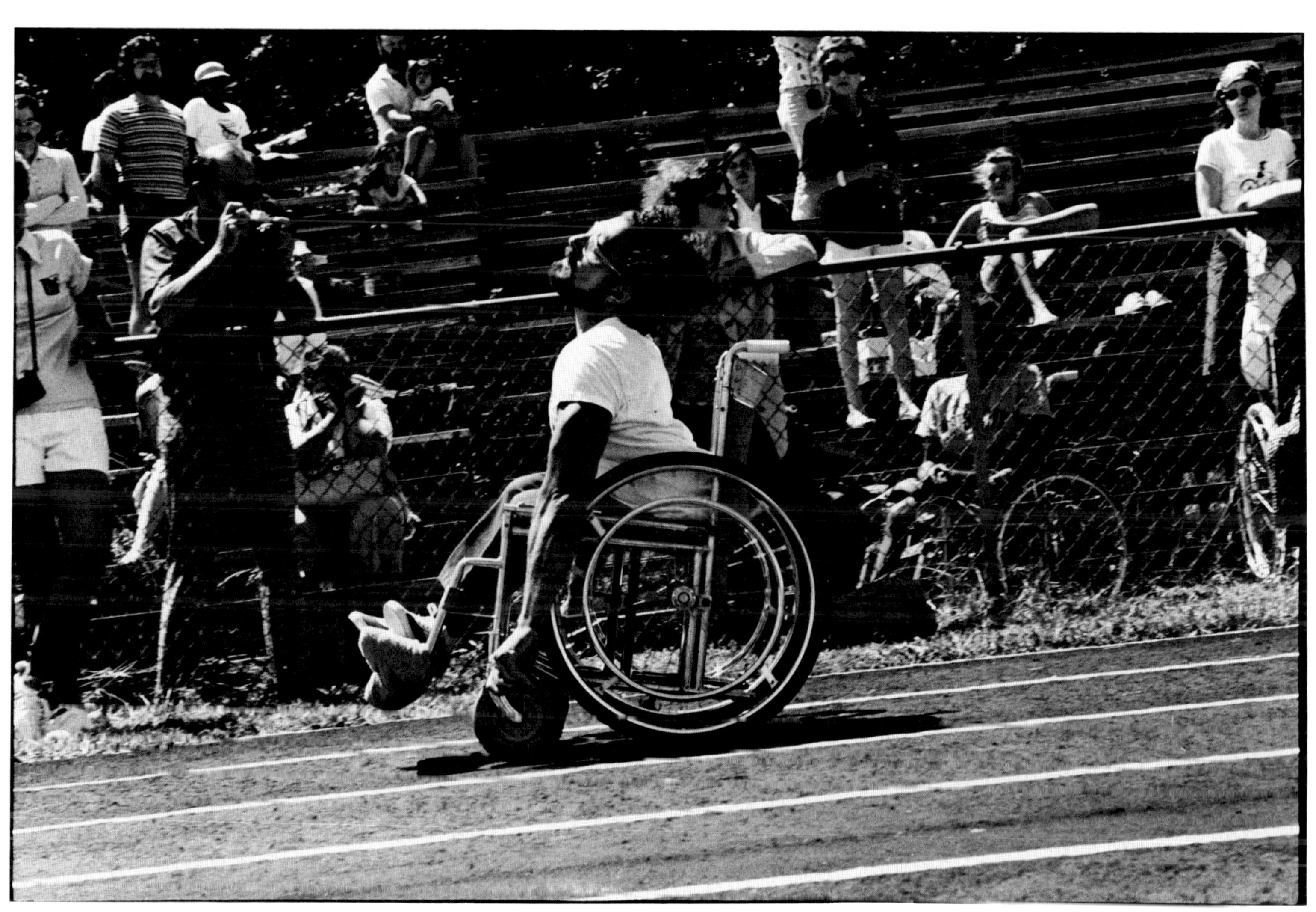

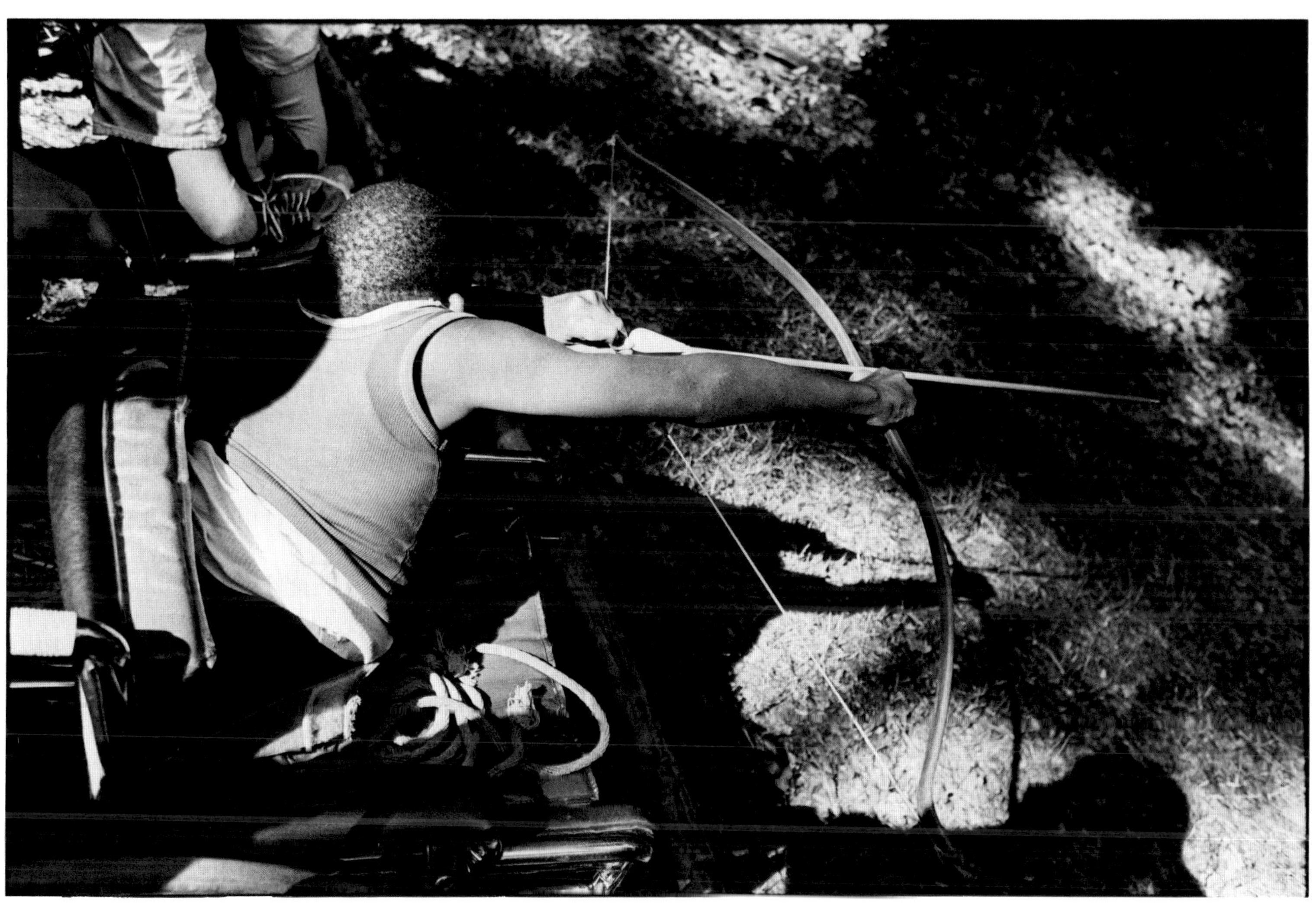

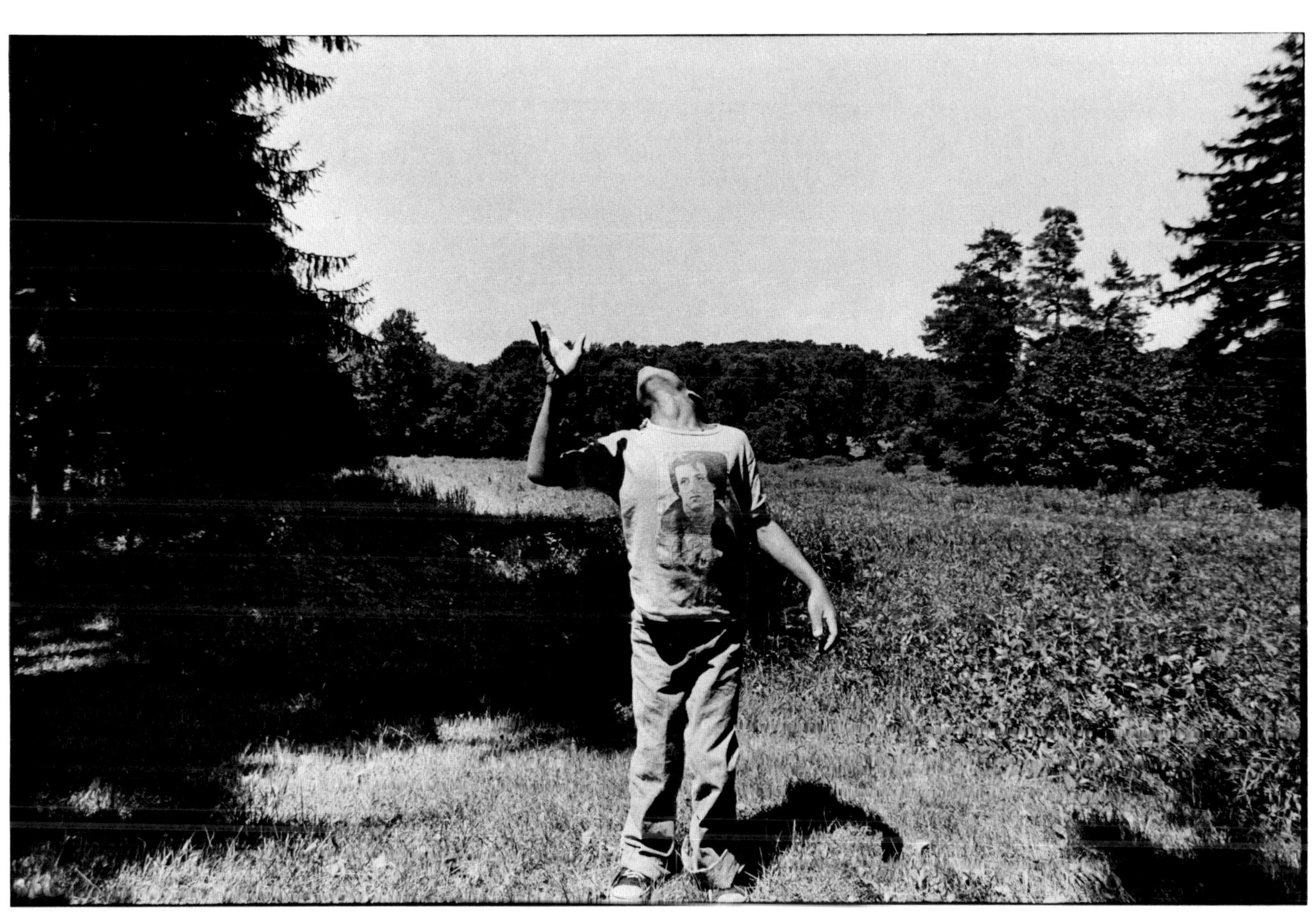

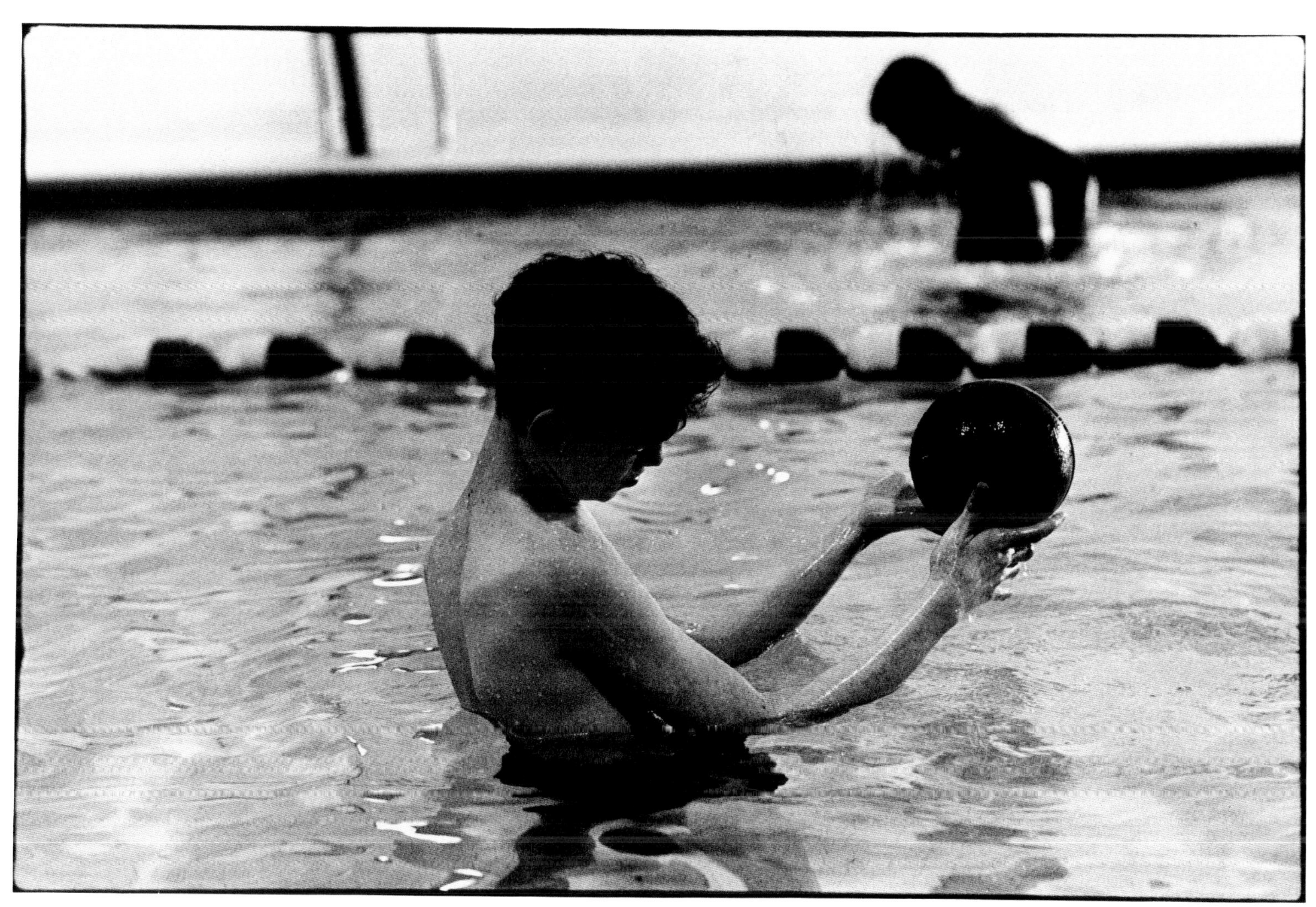

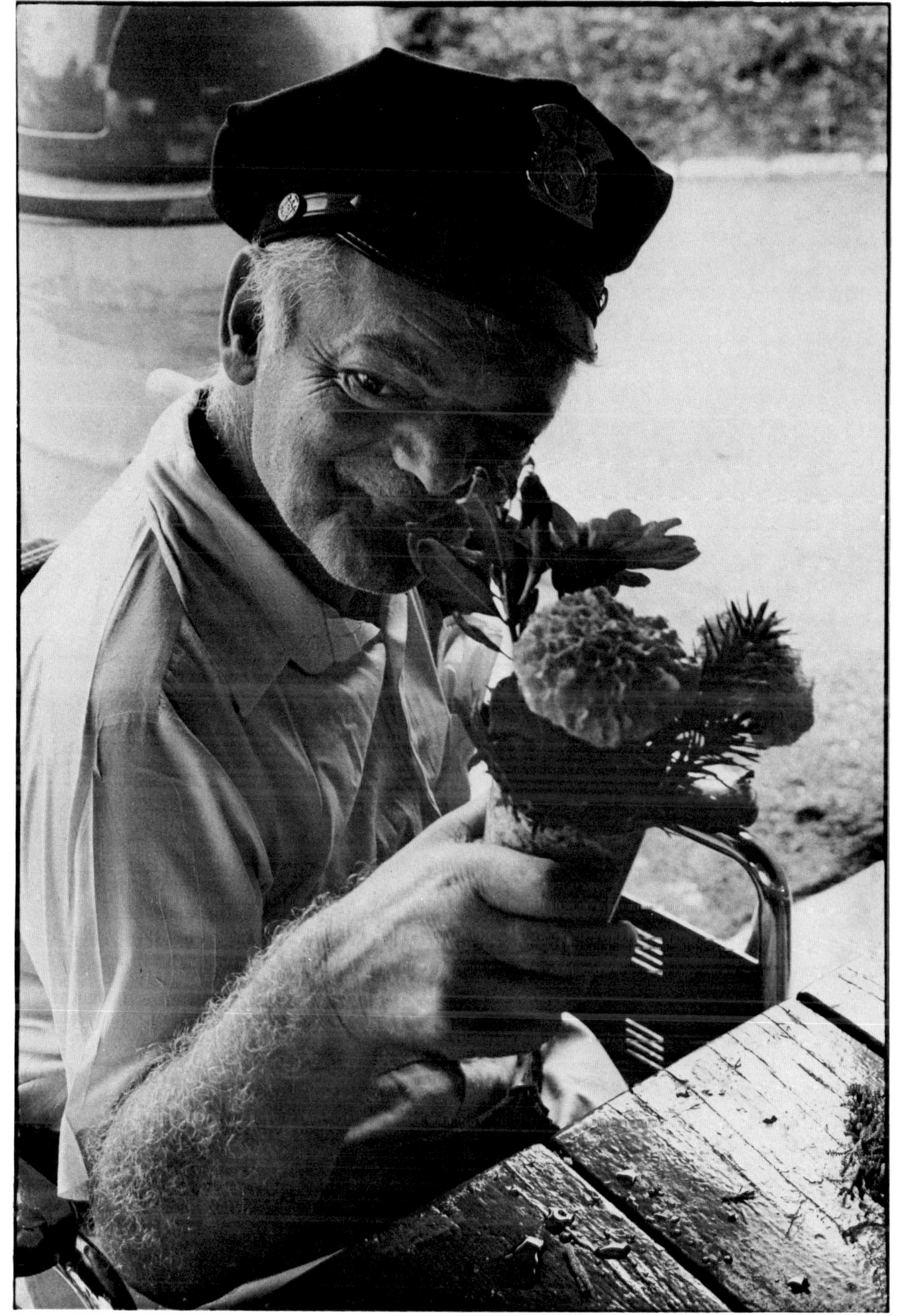

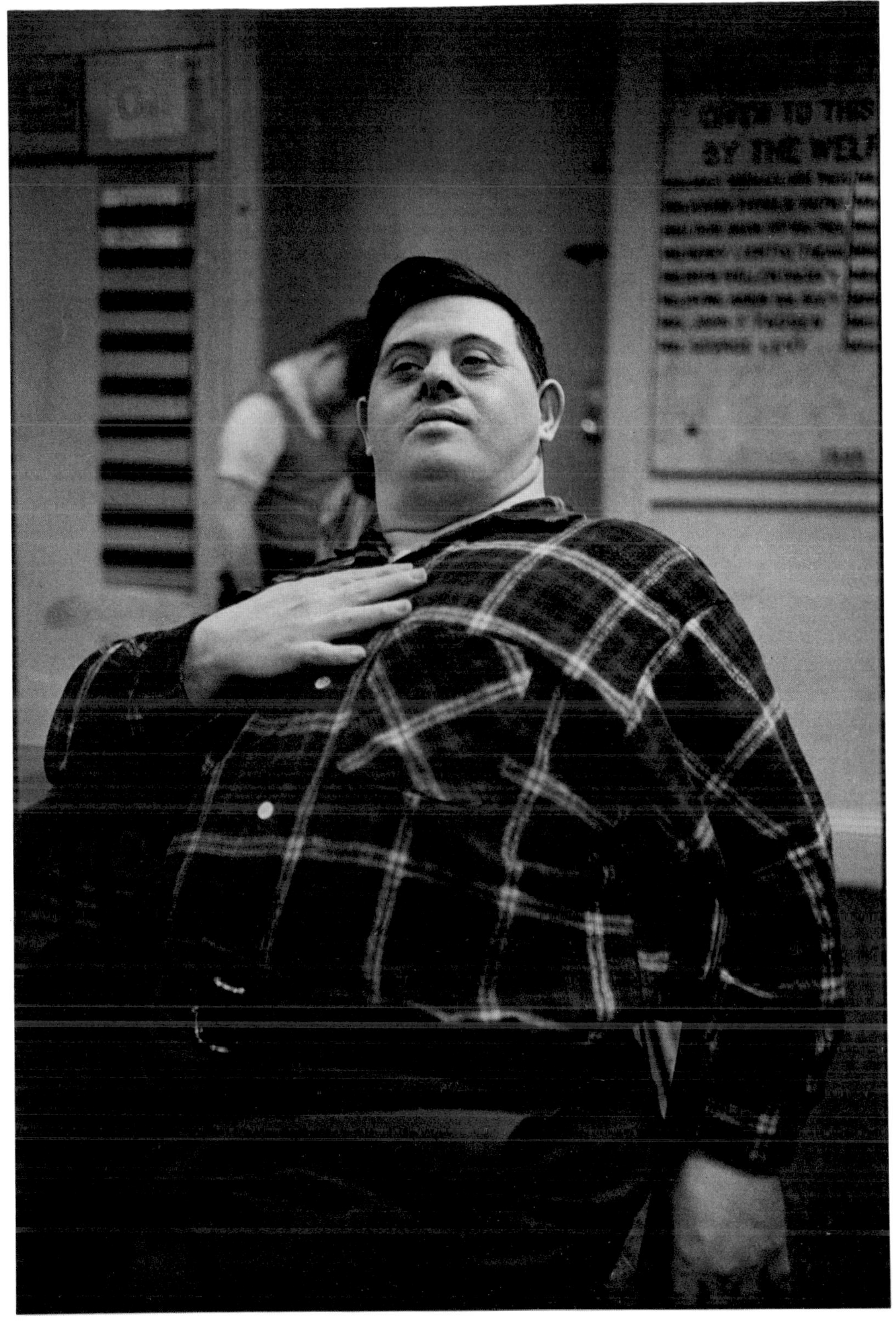

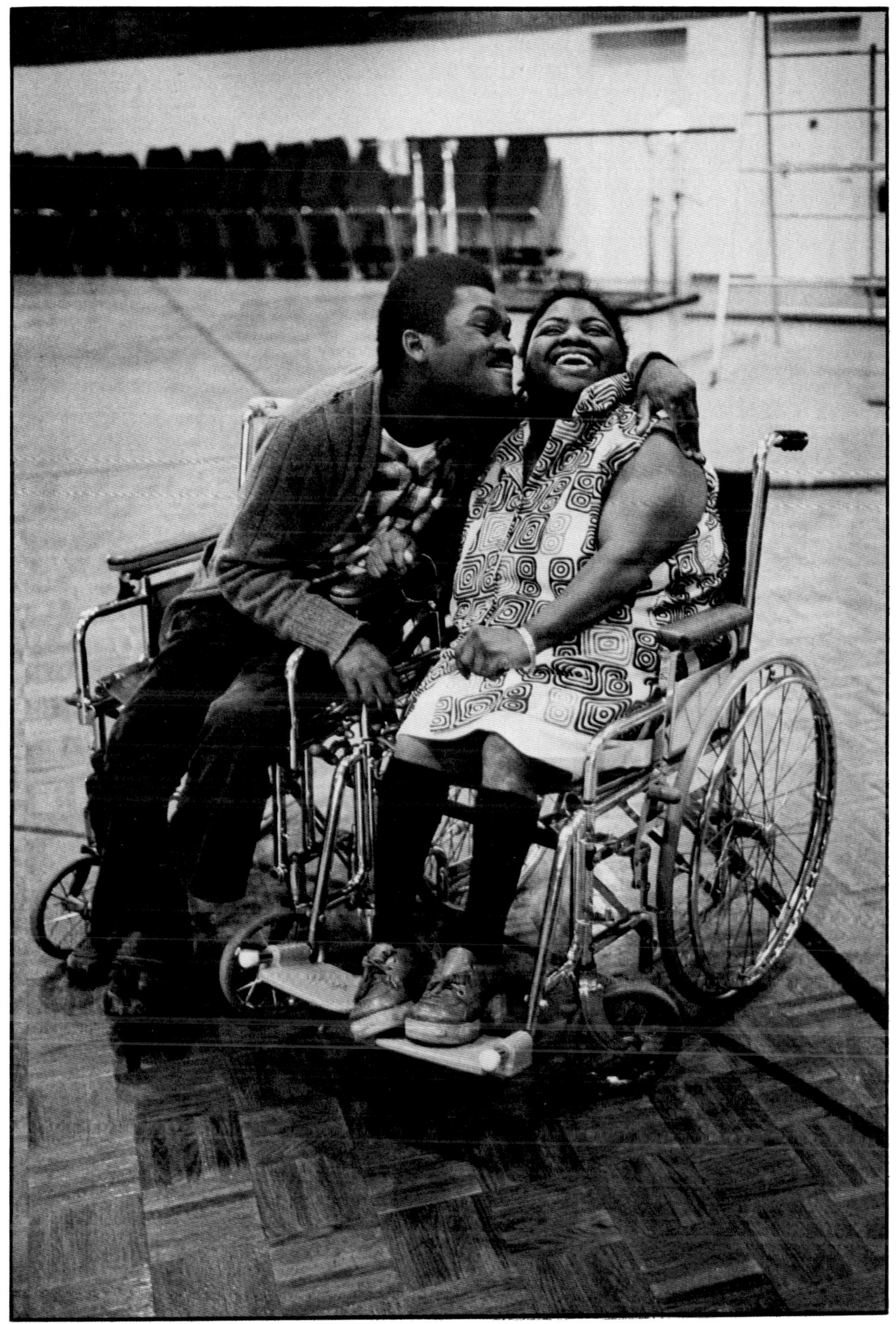

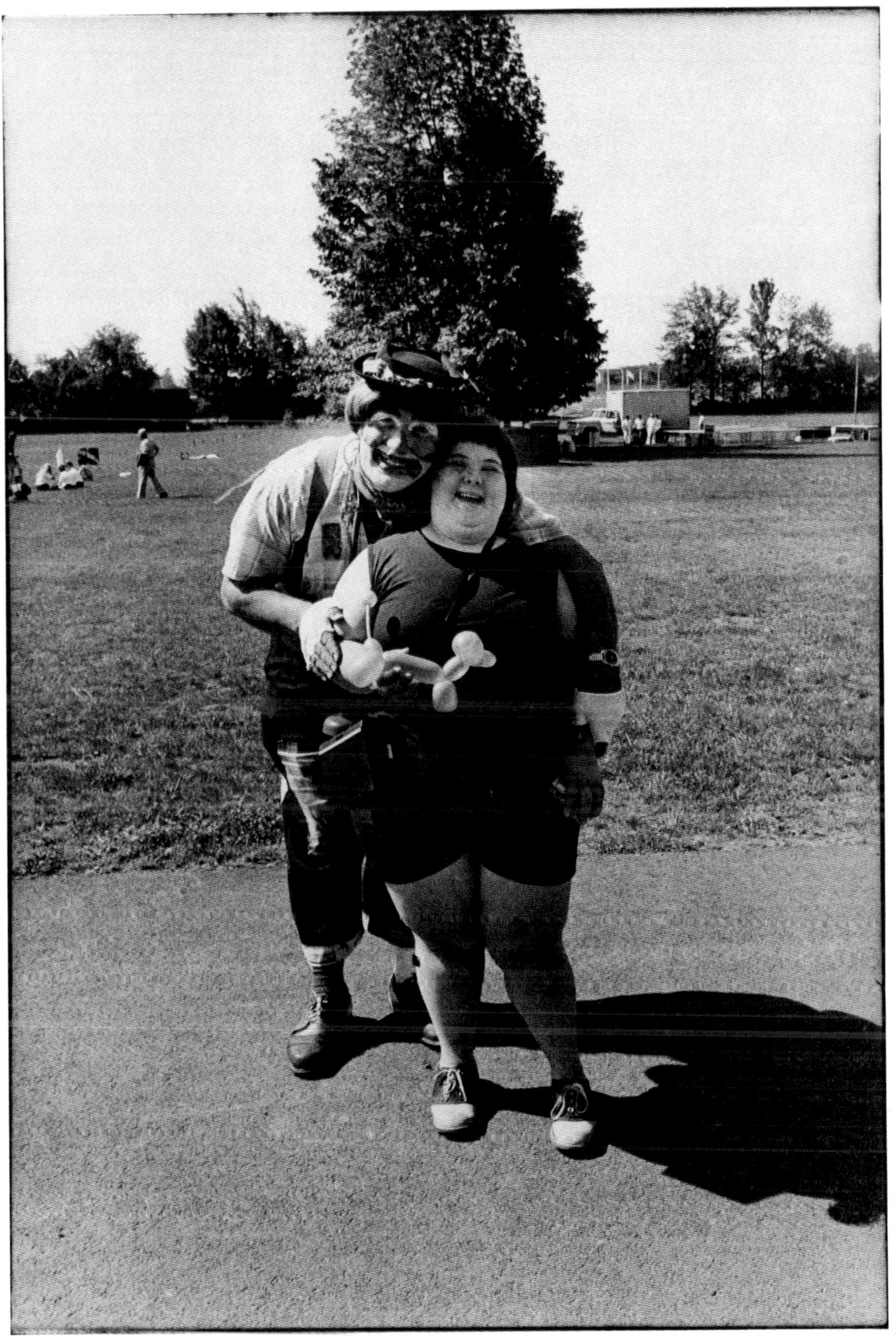

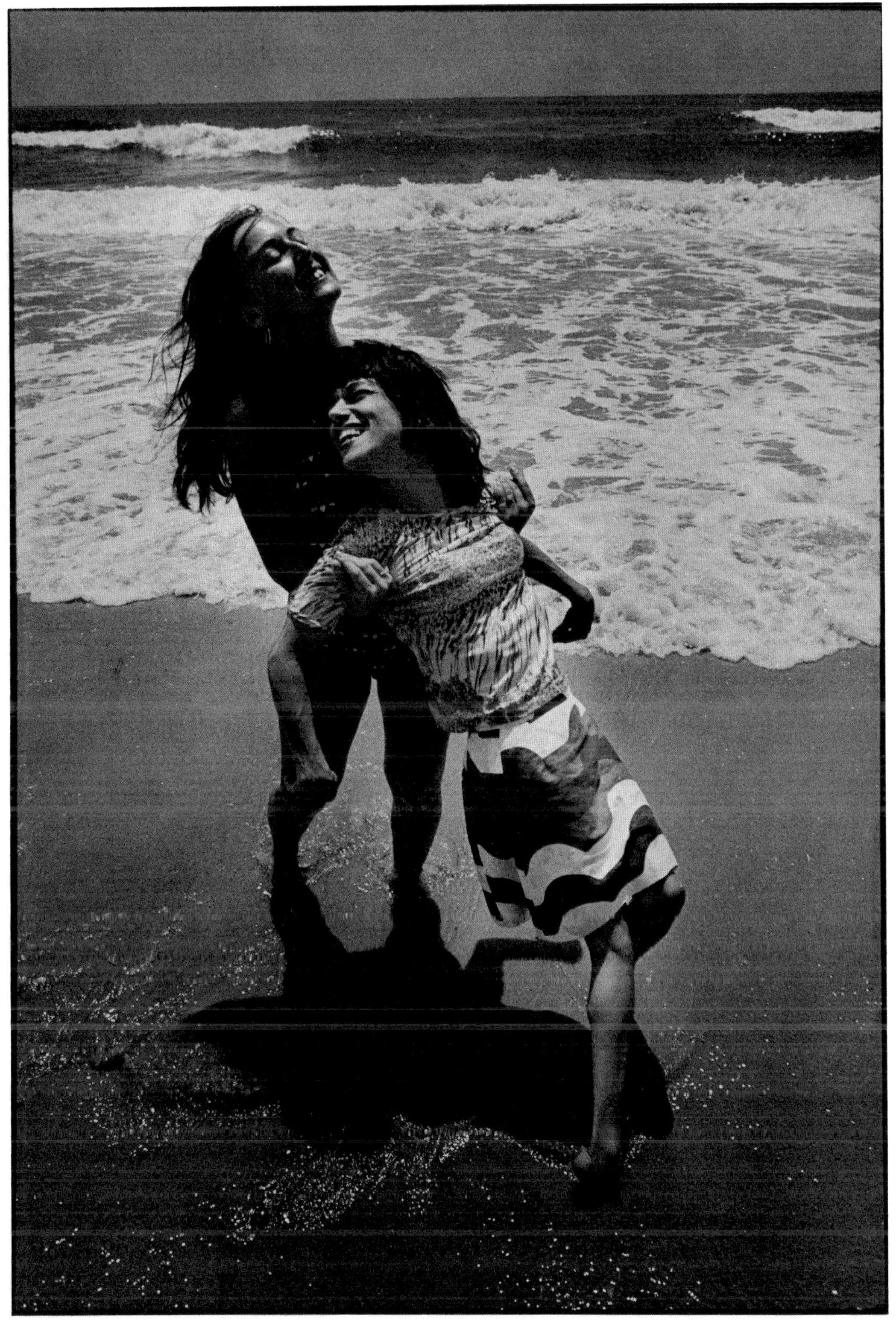

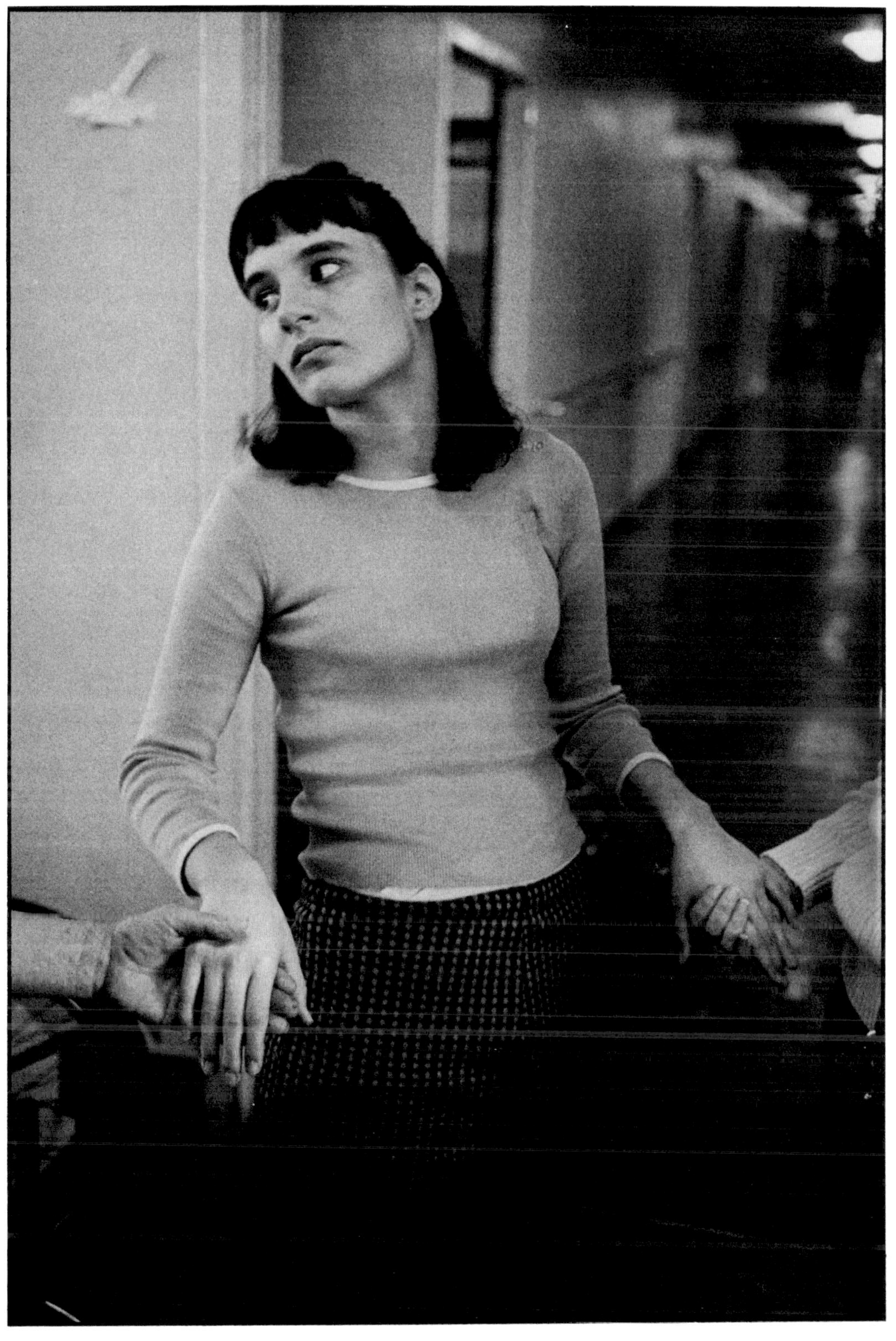

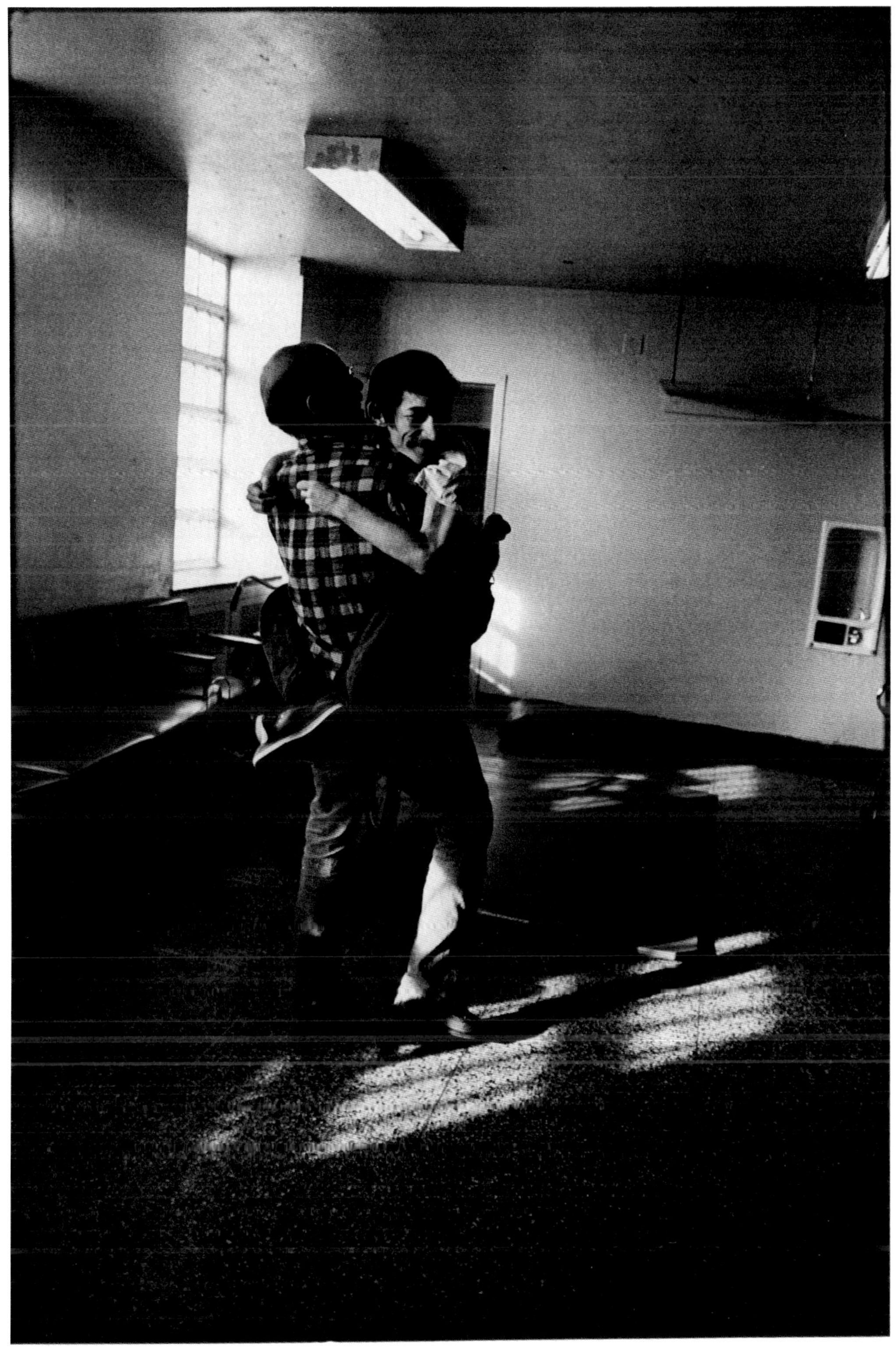

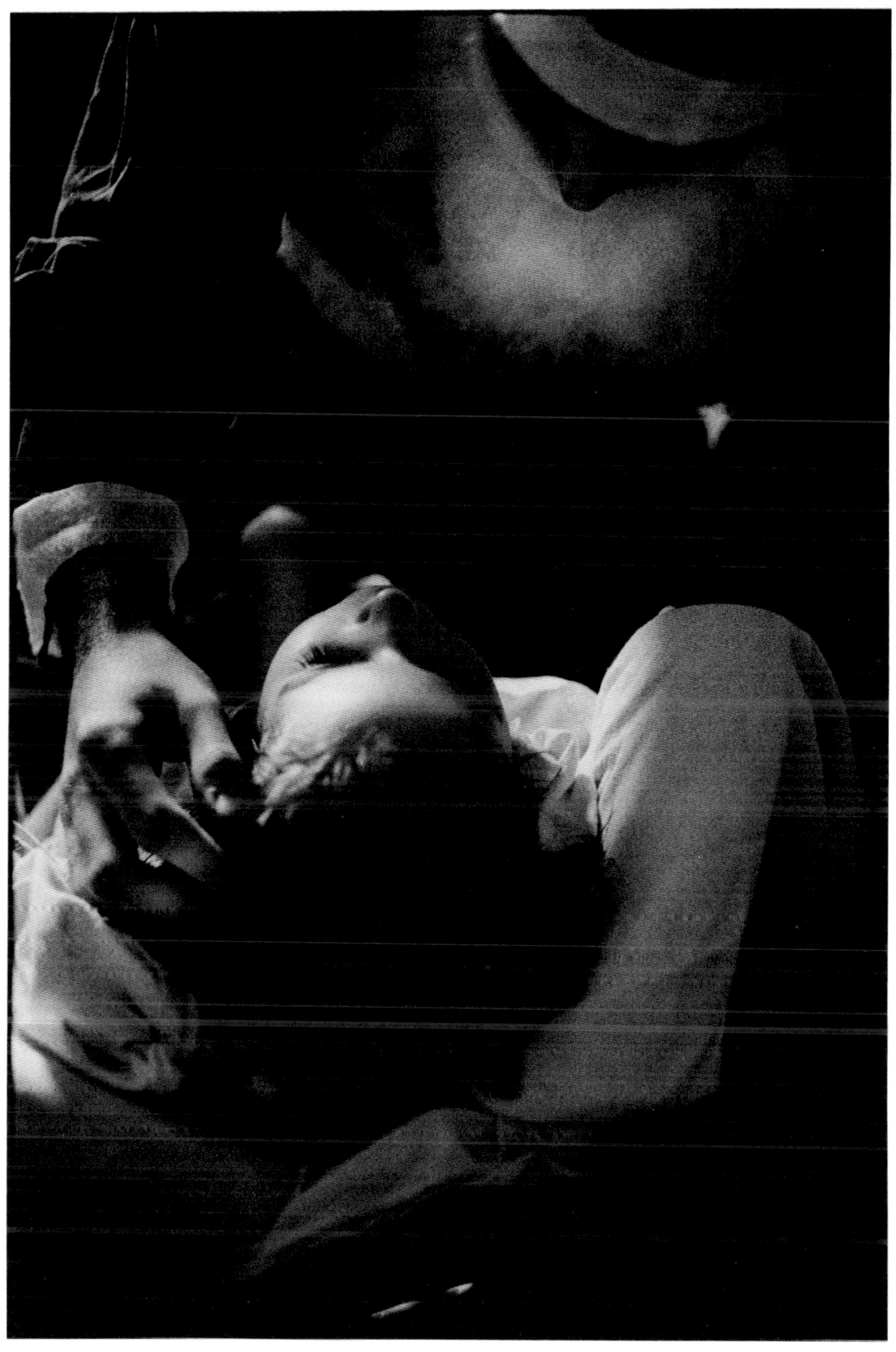

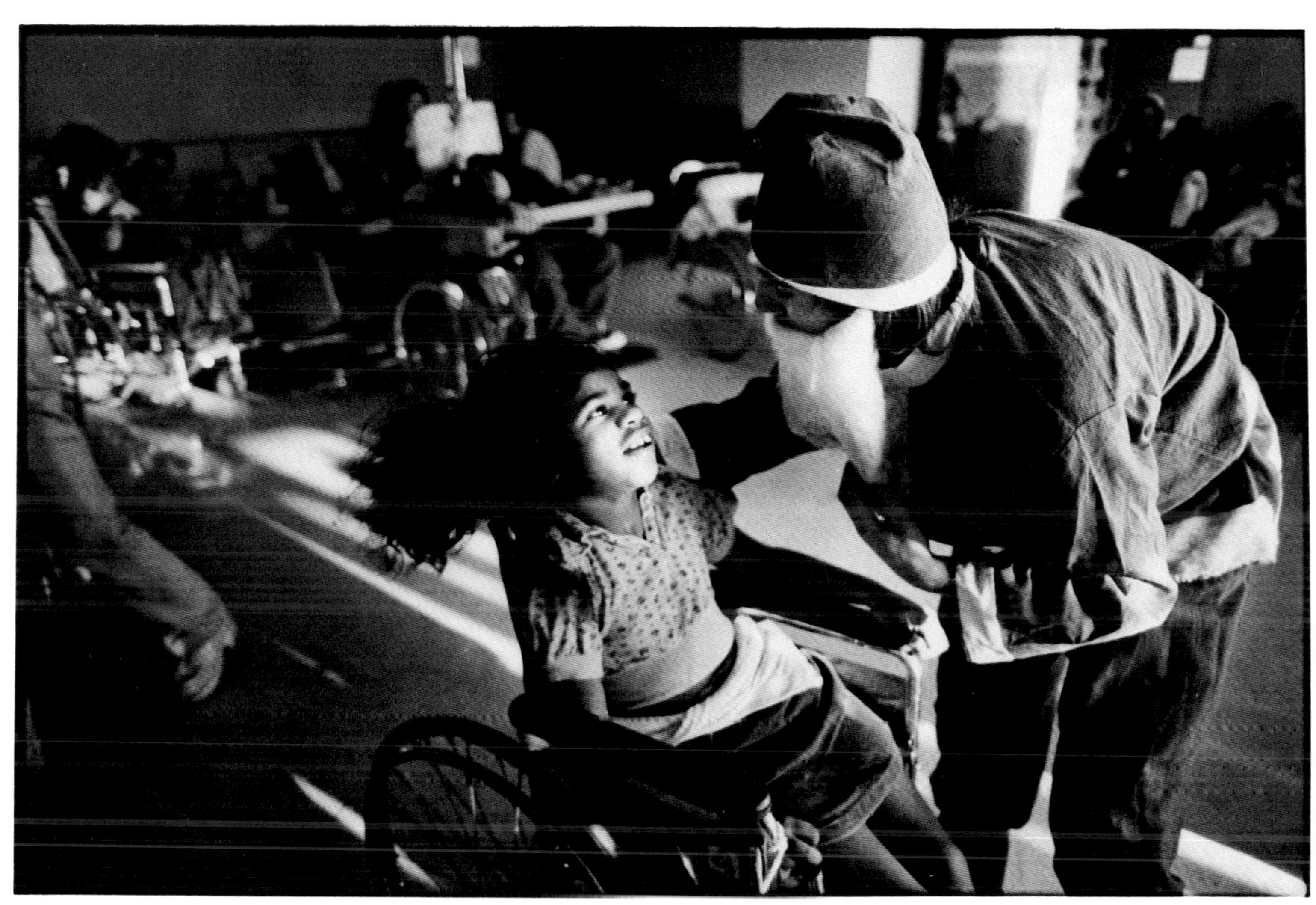

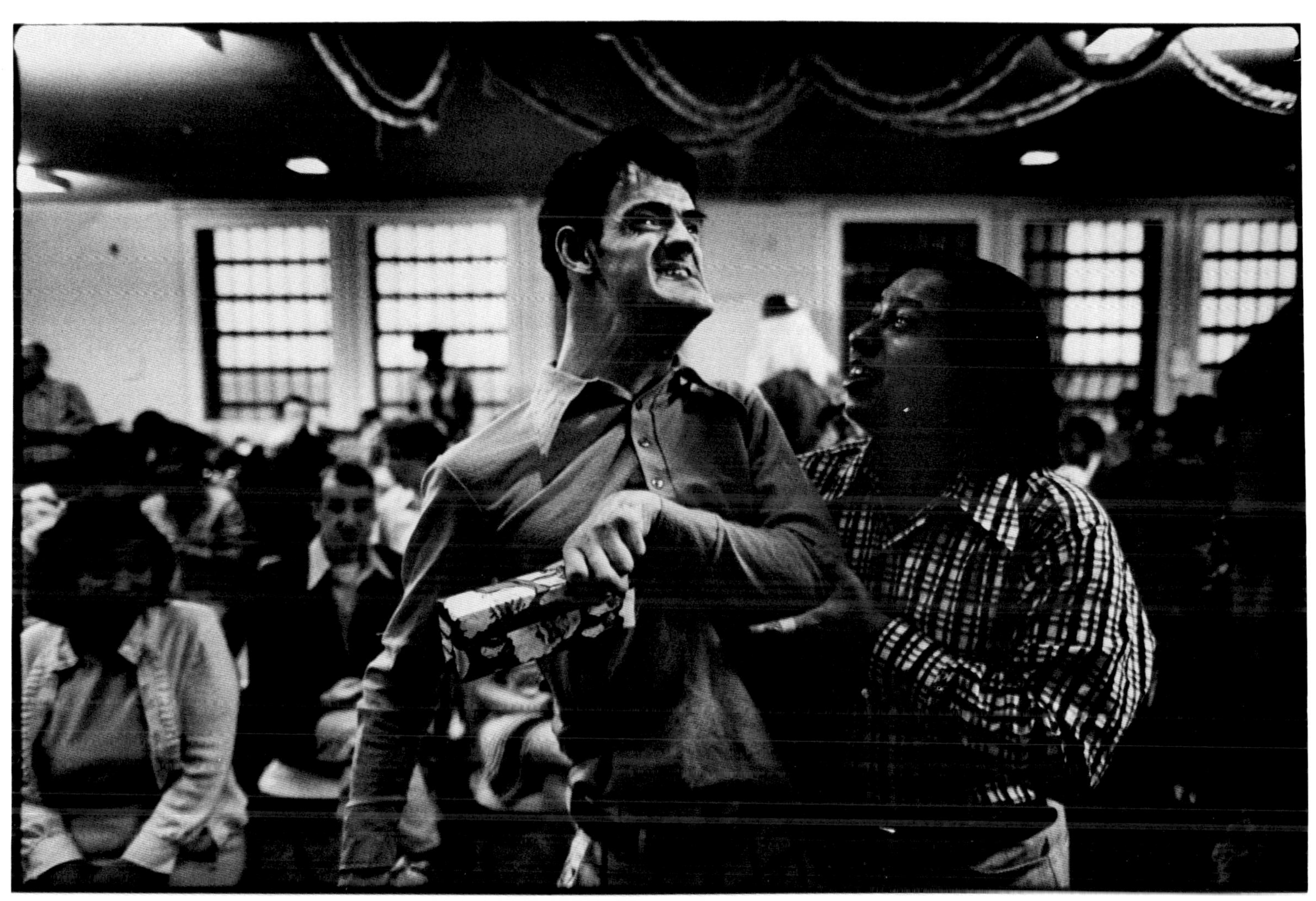

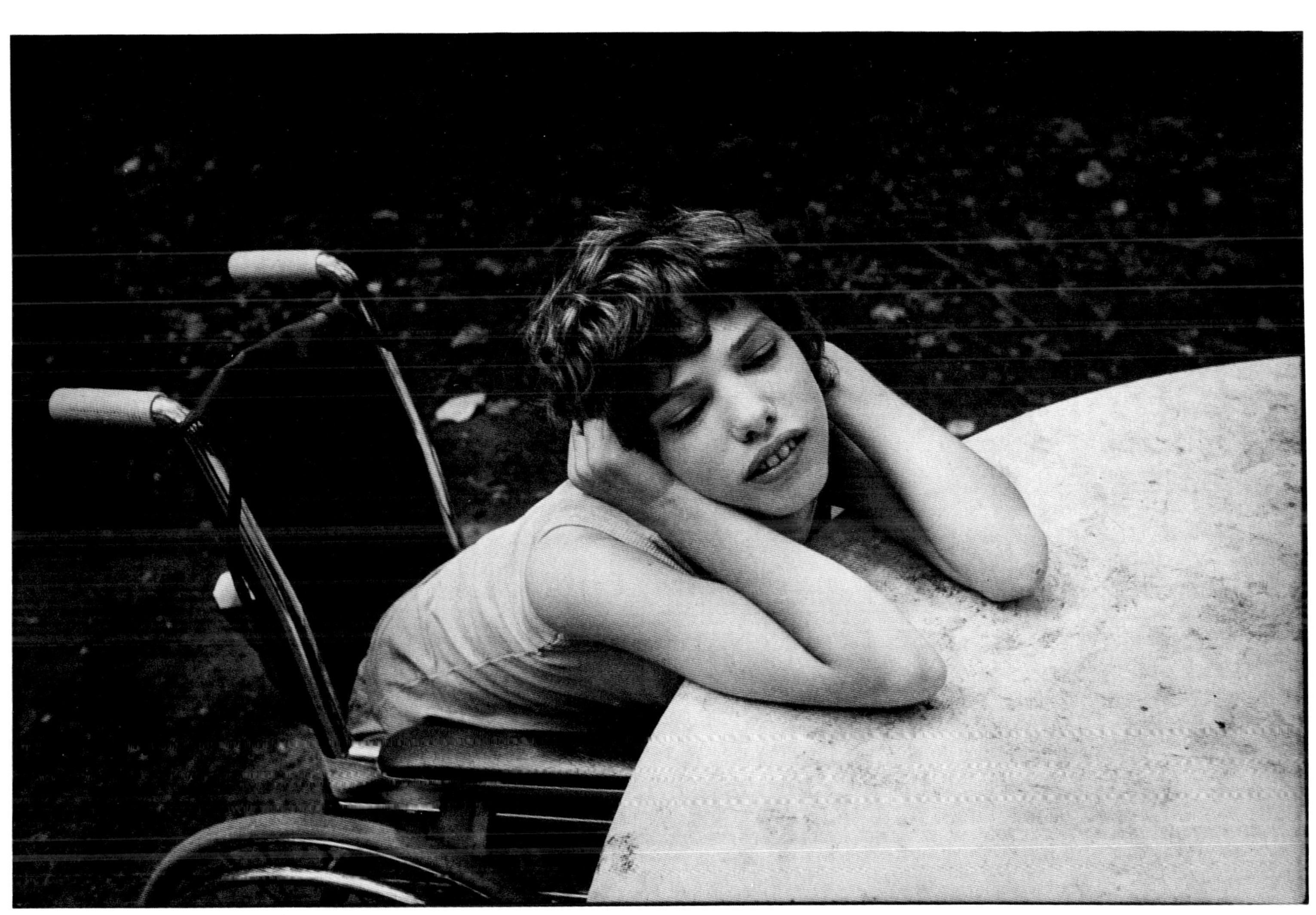

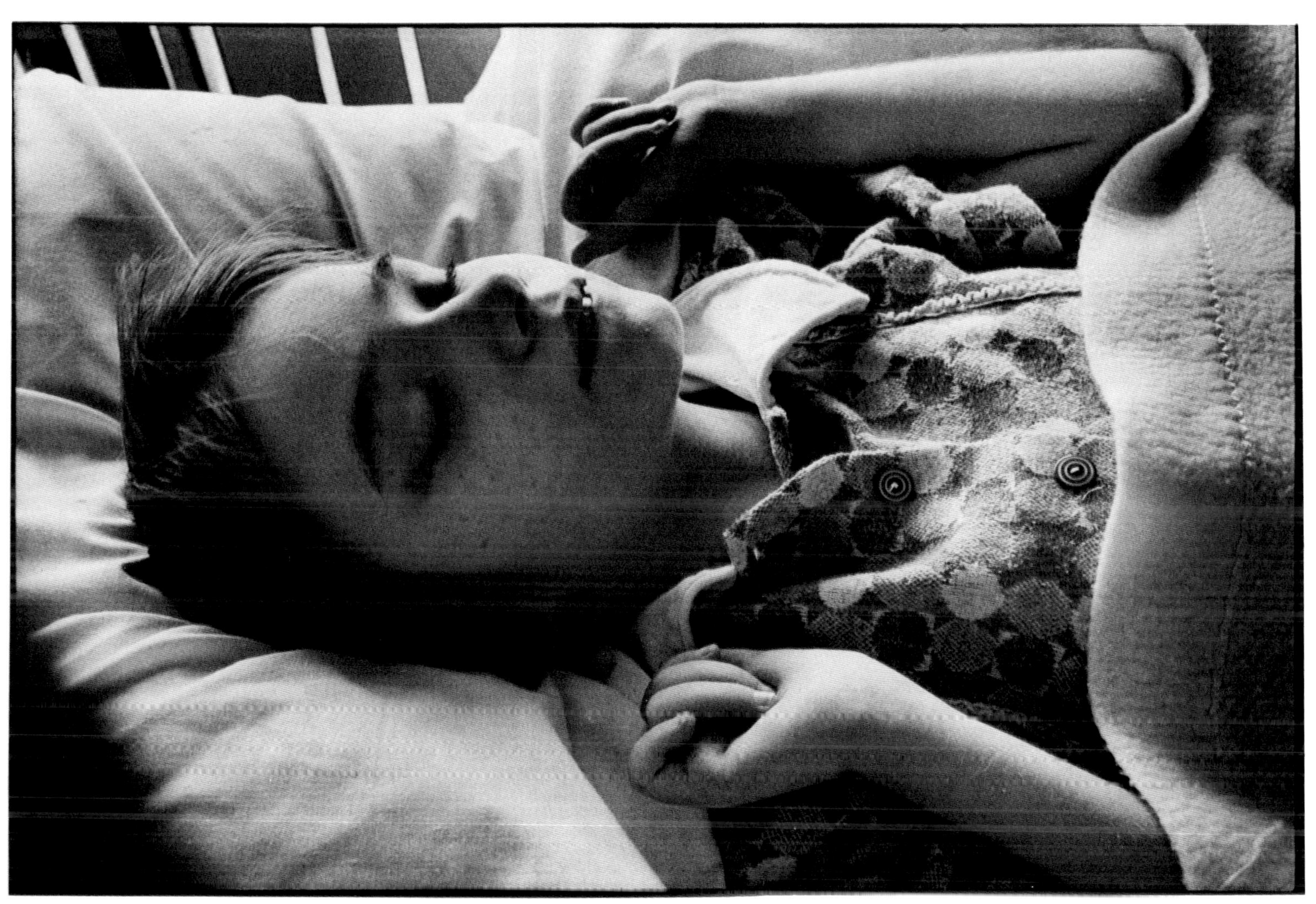

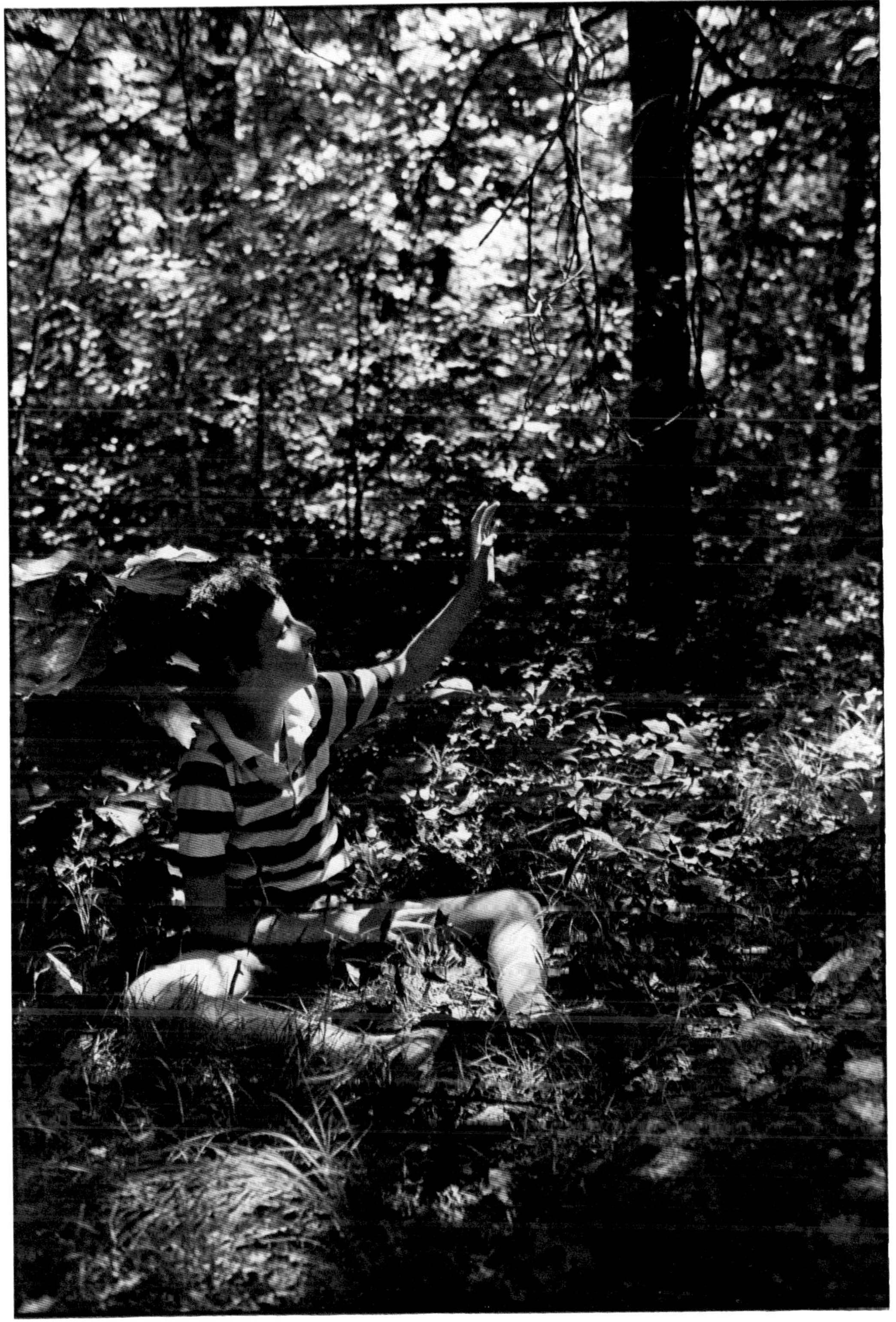

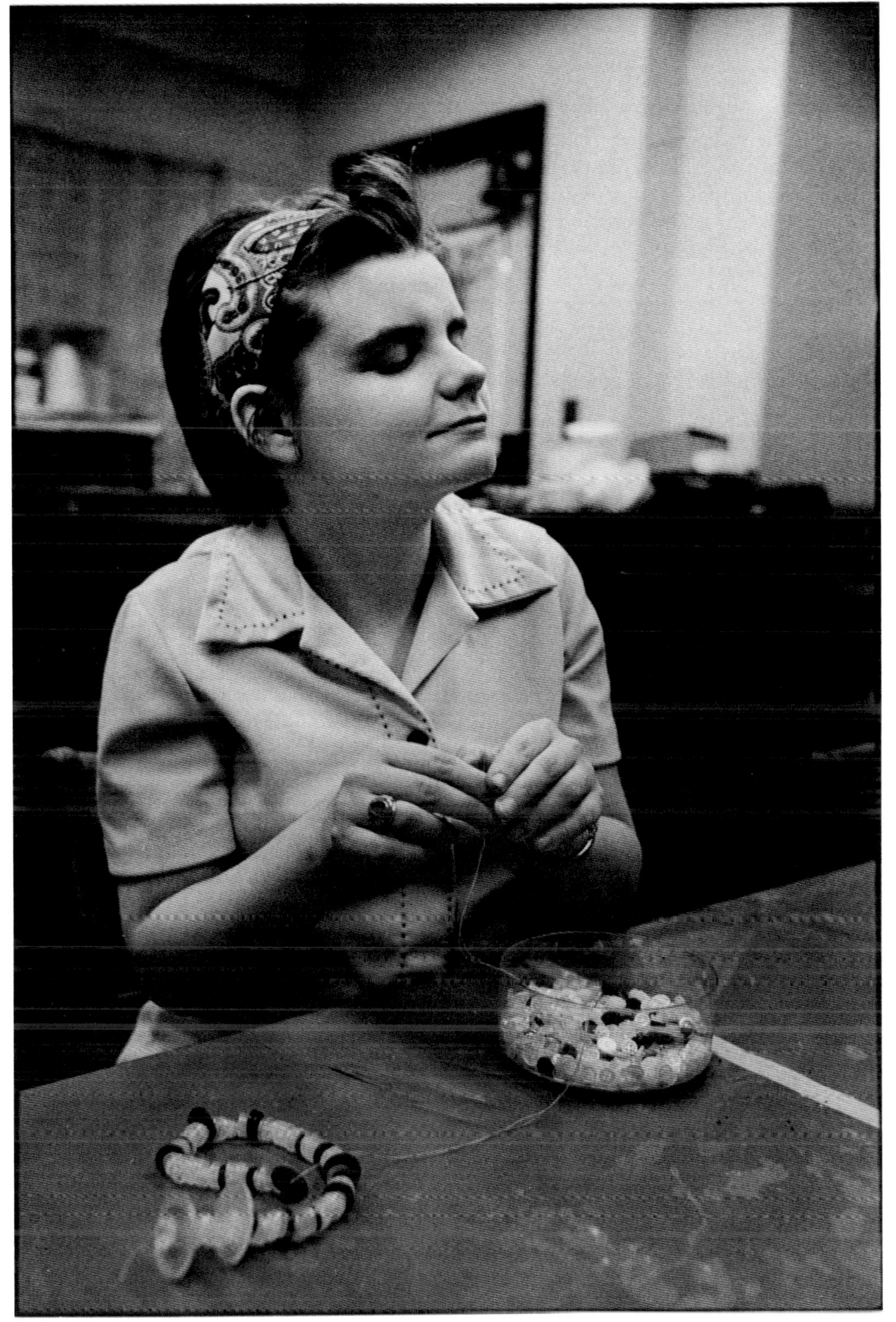

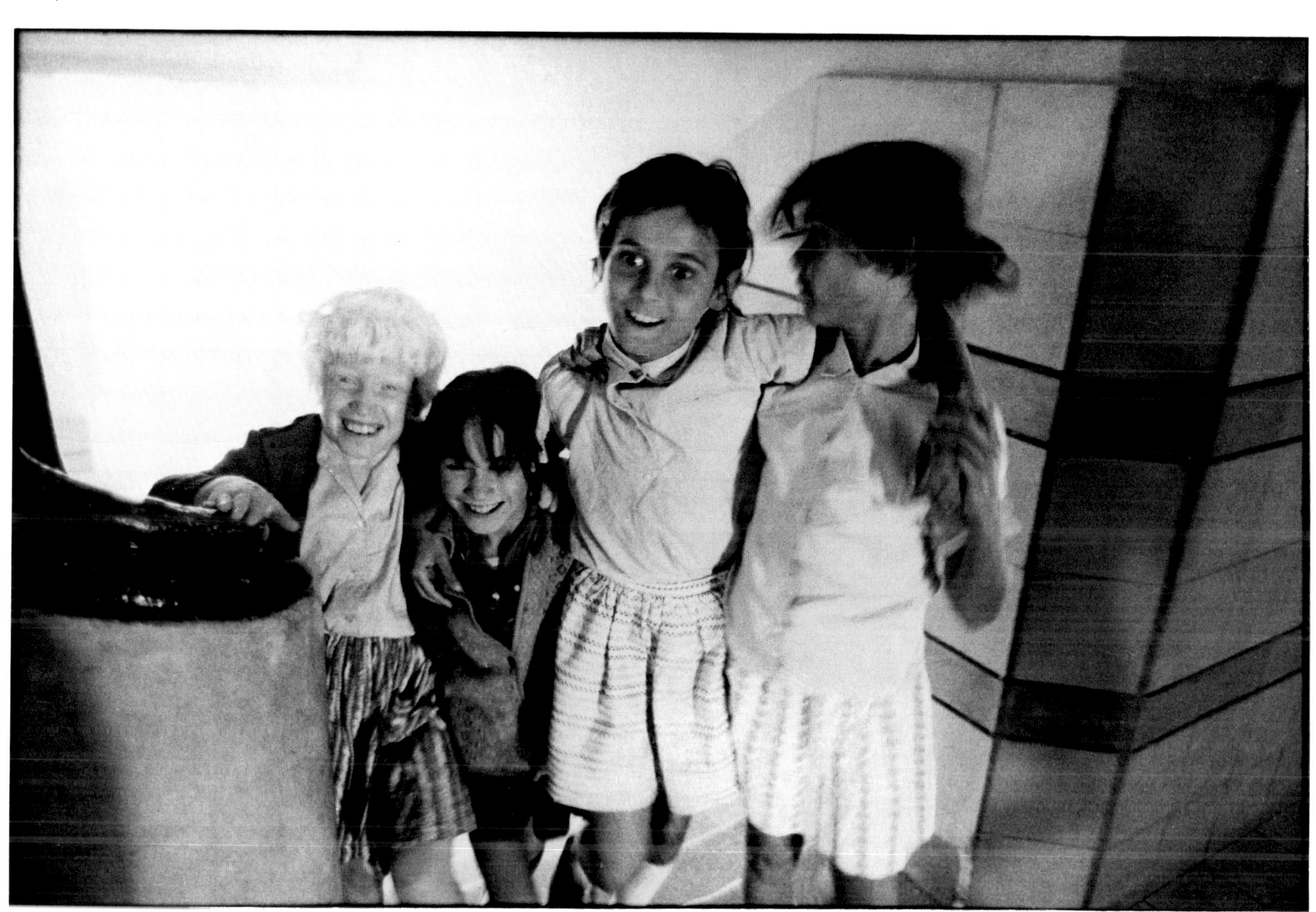

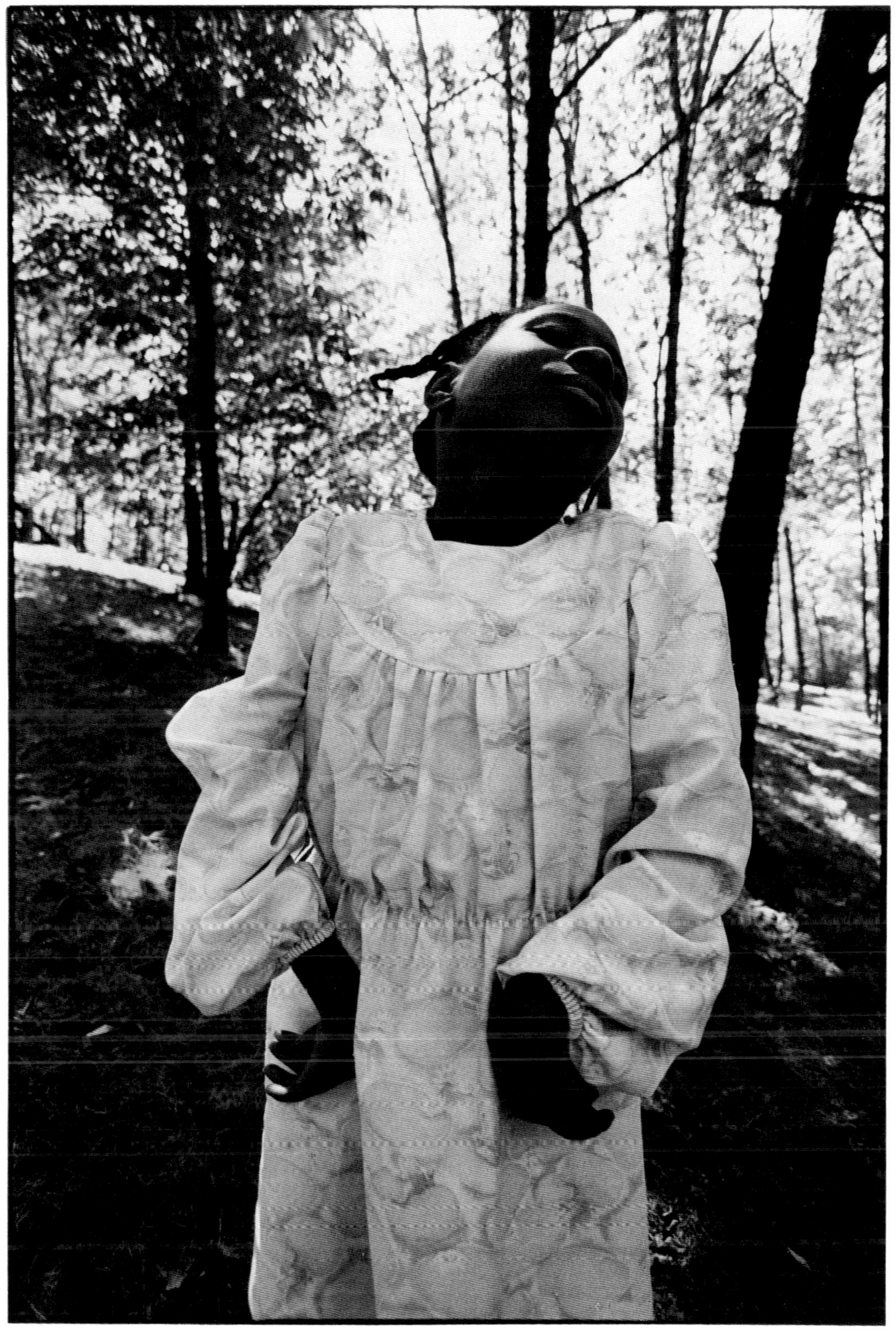

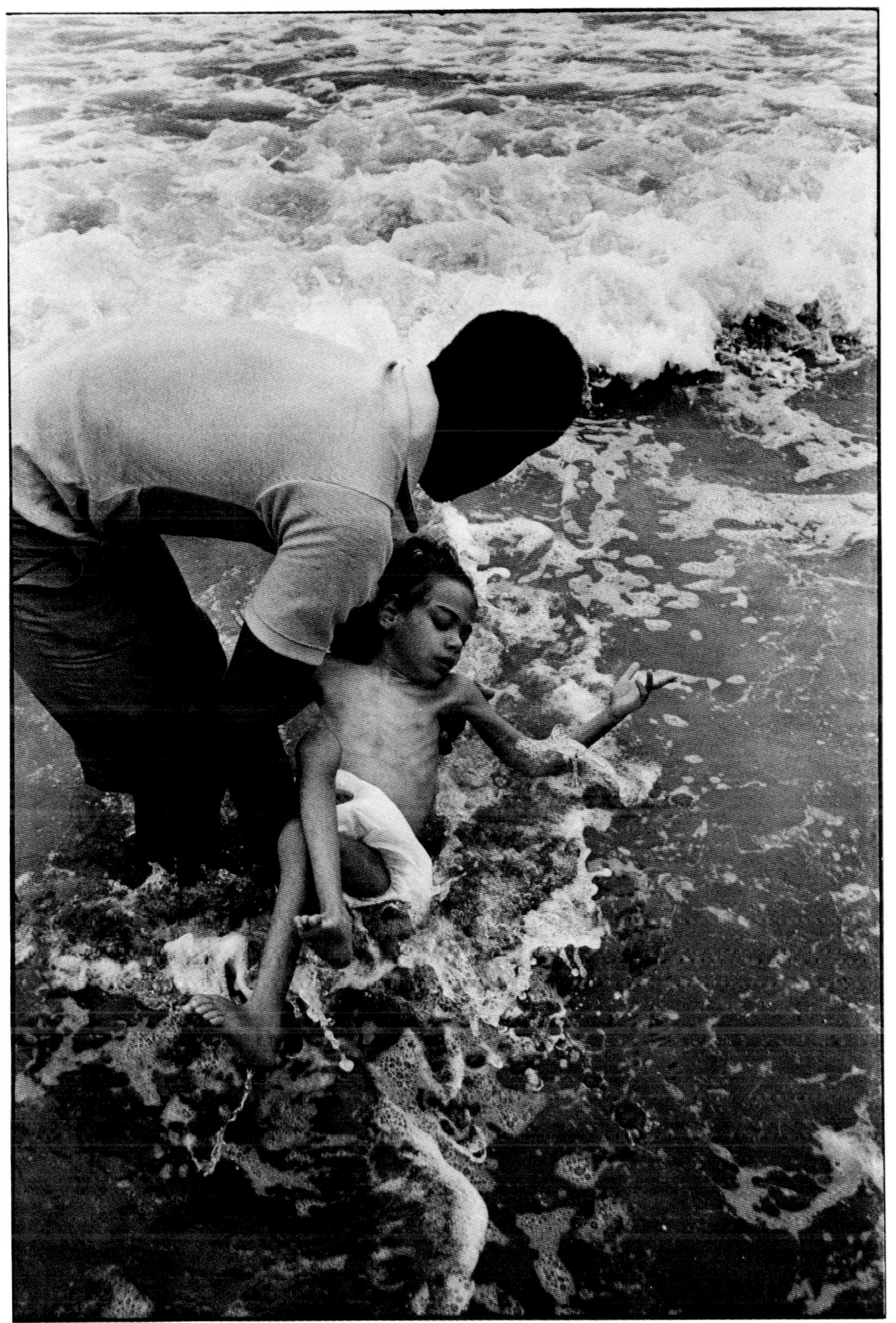

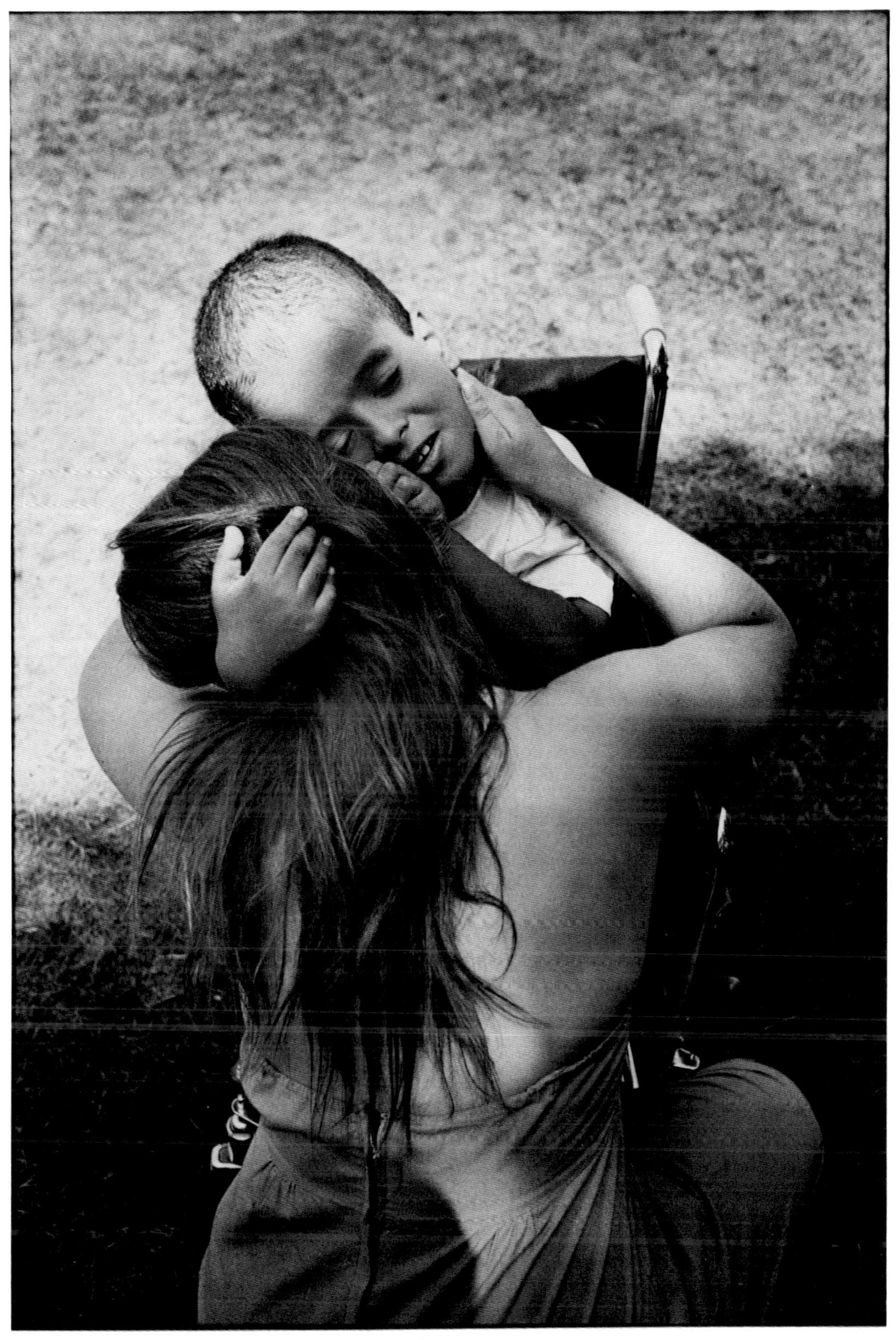

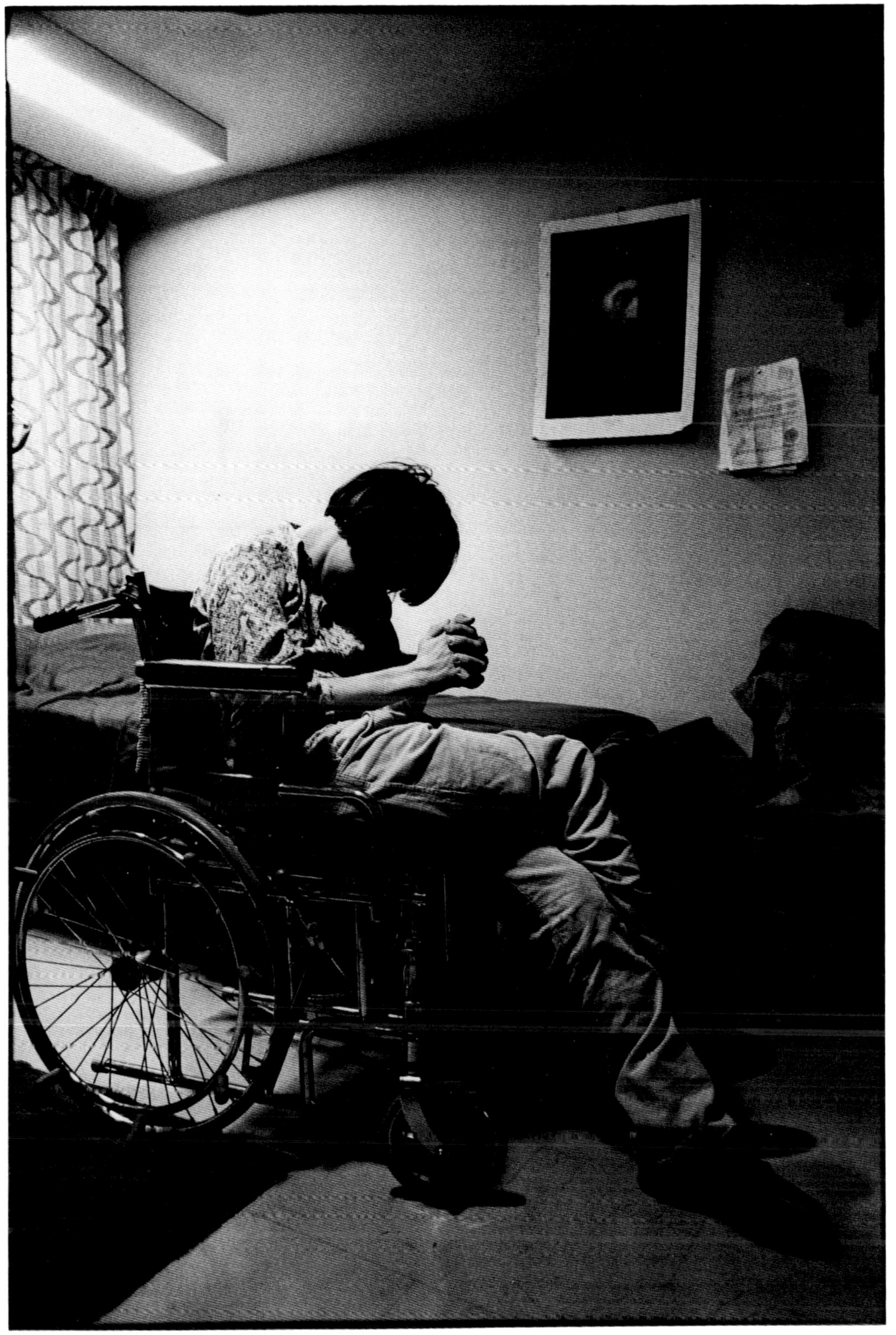

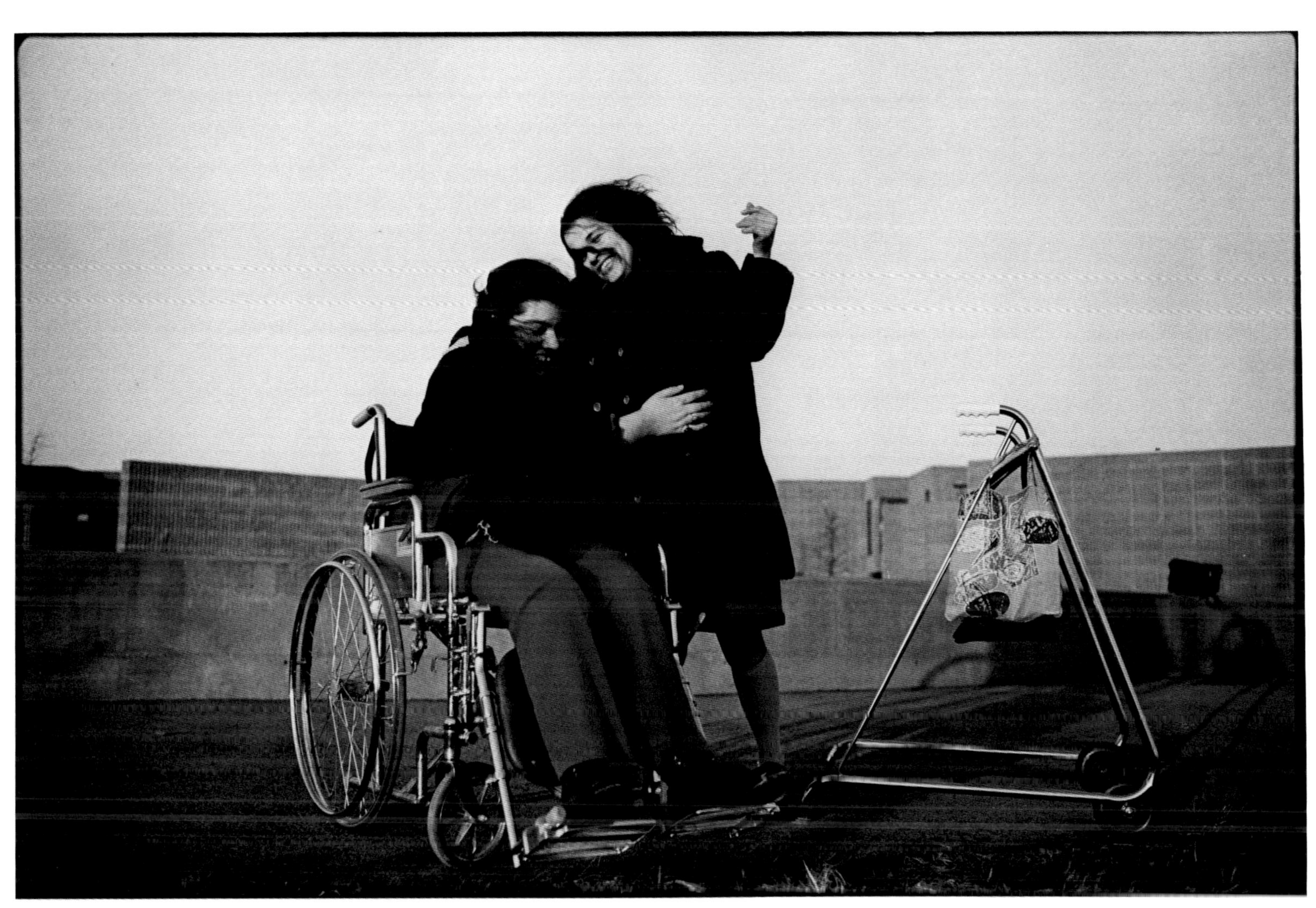

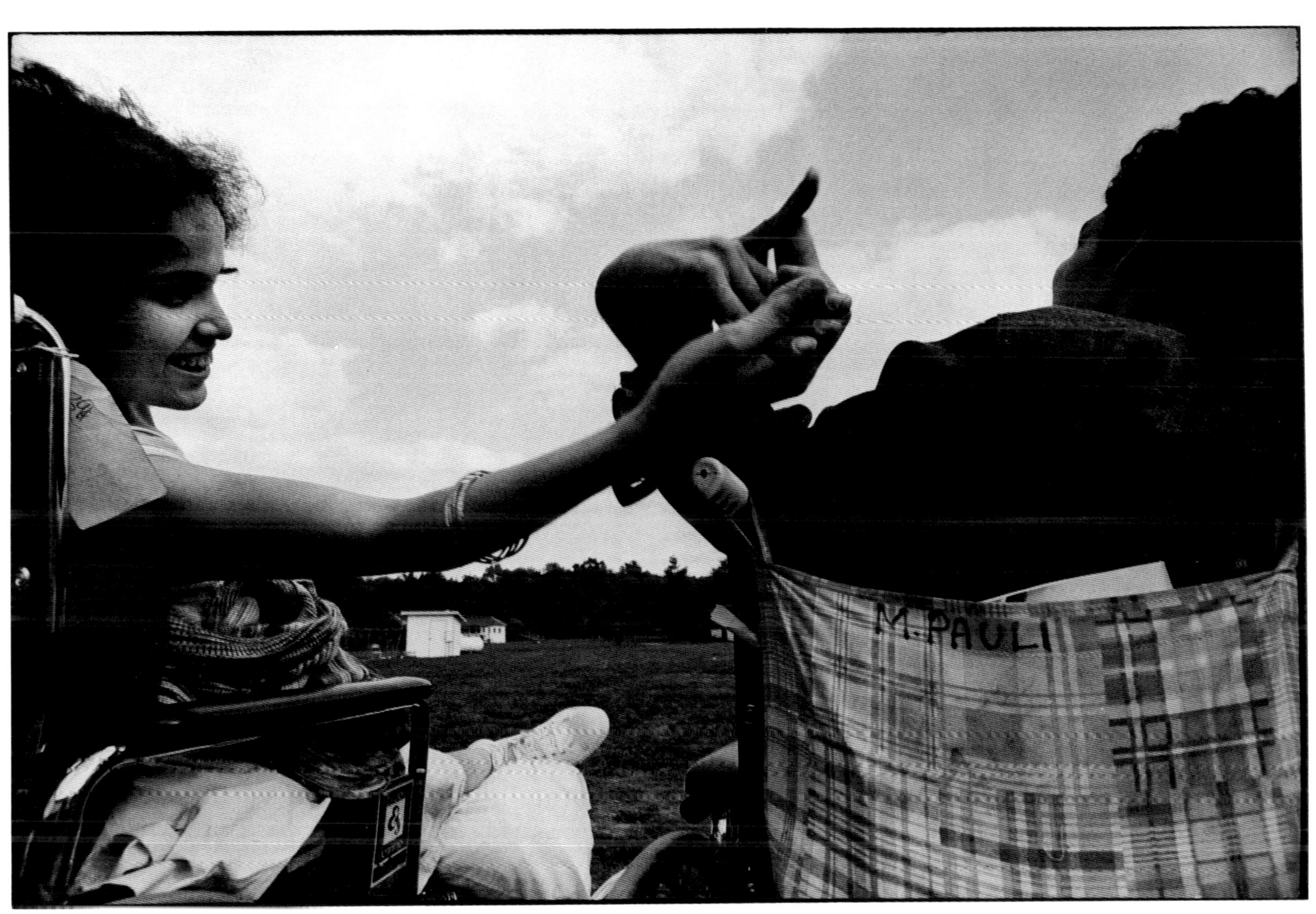
M. PAULI

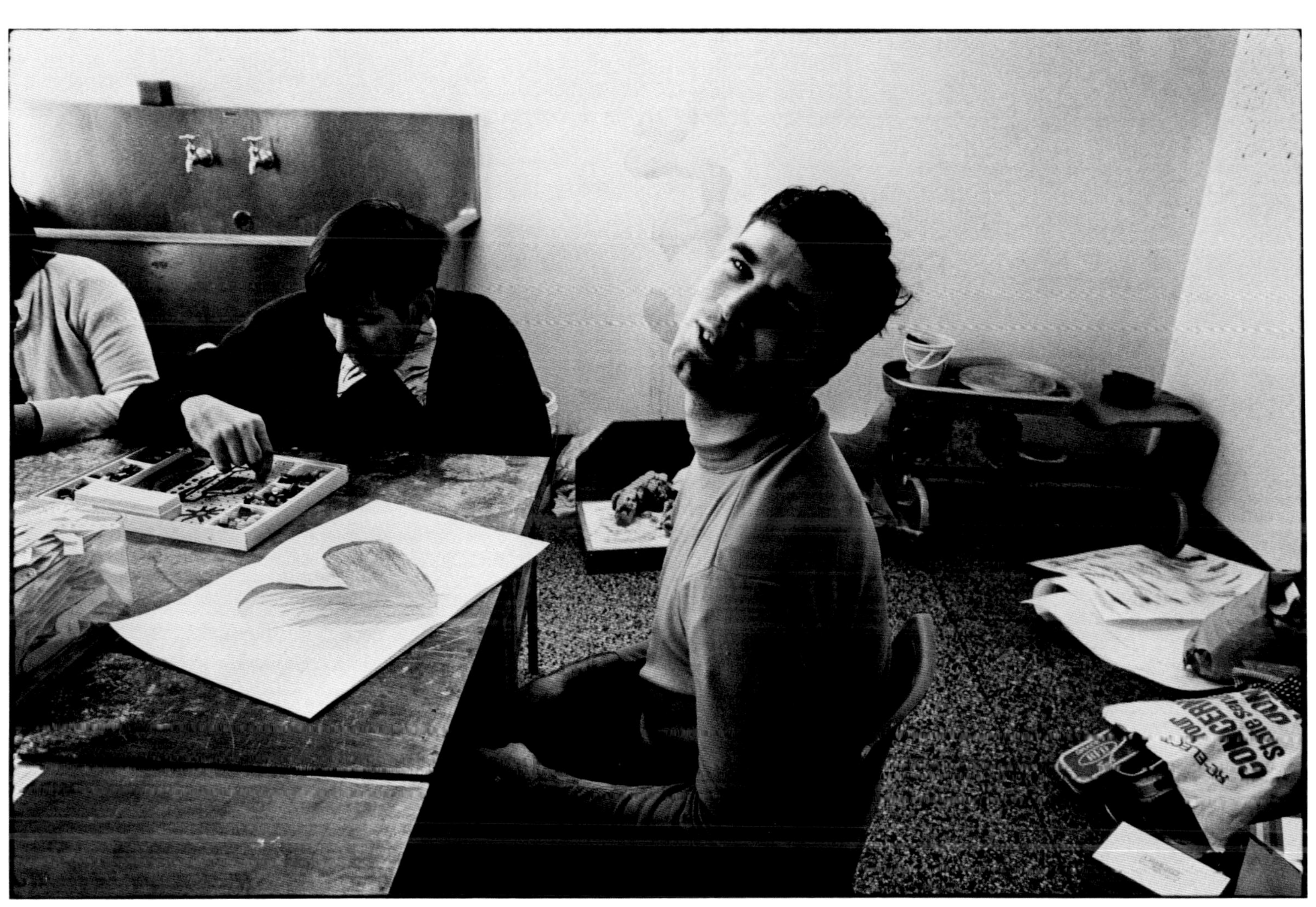

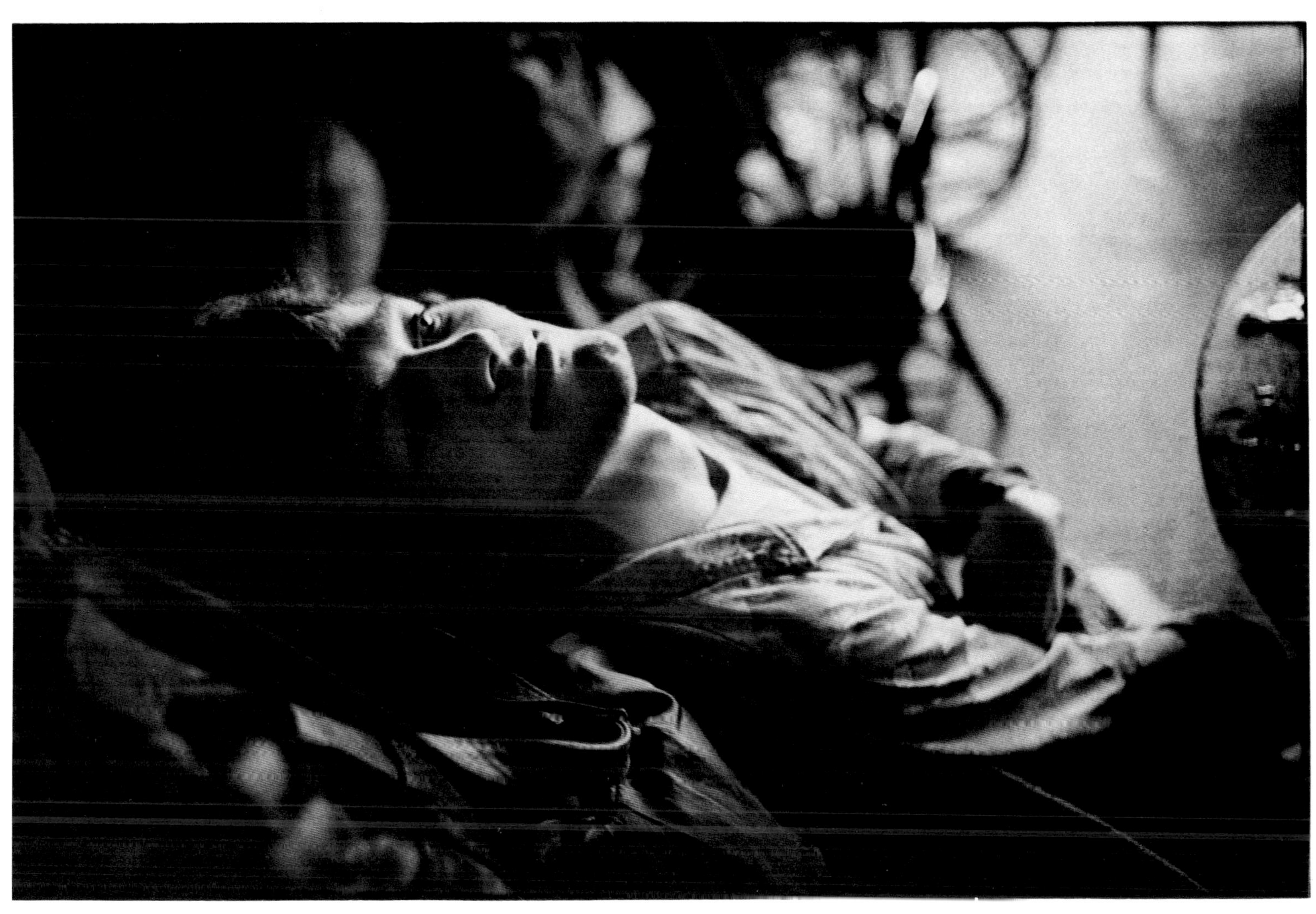

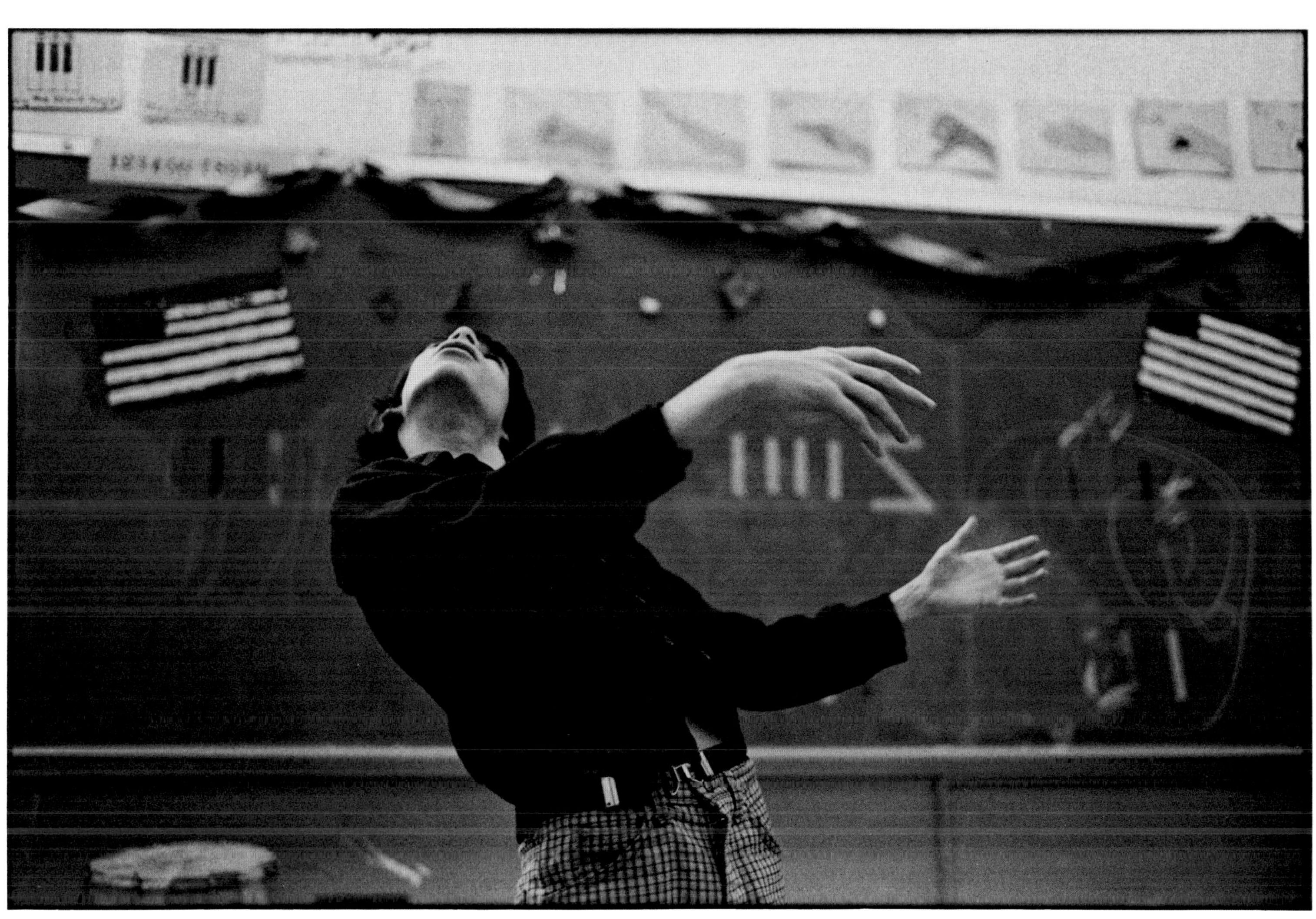

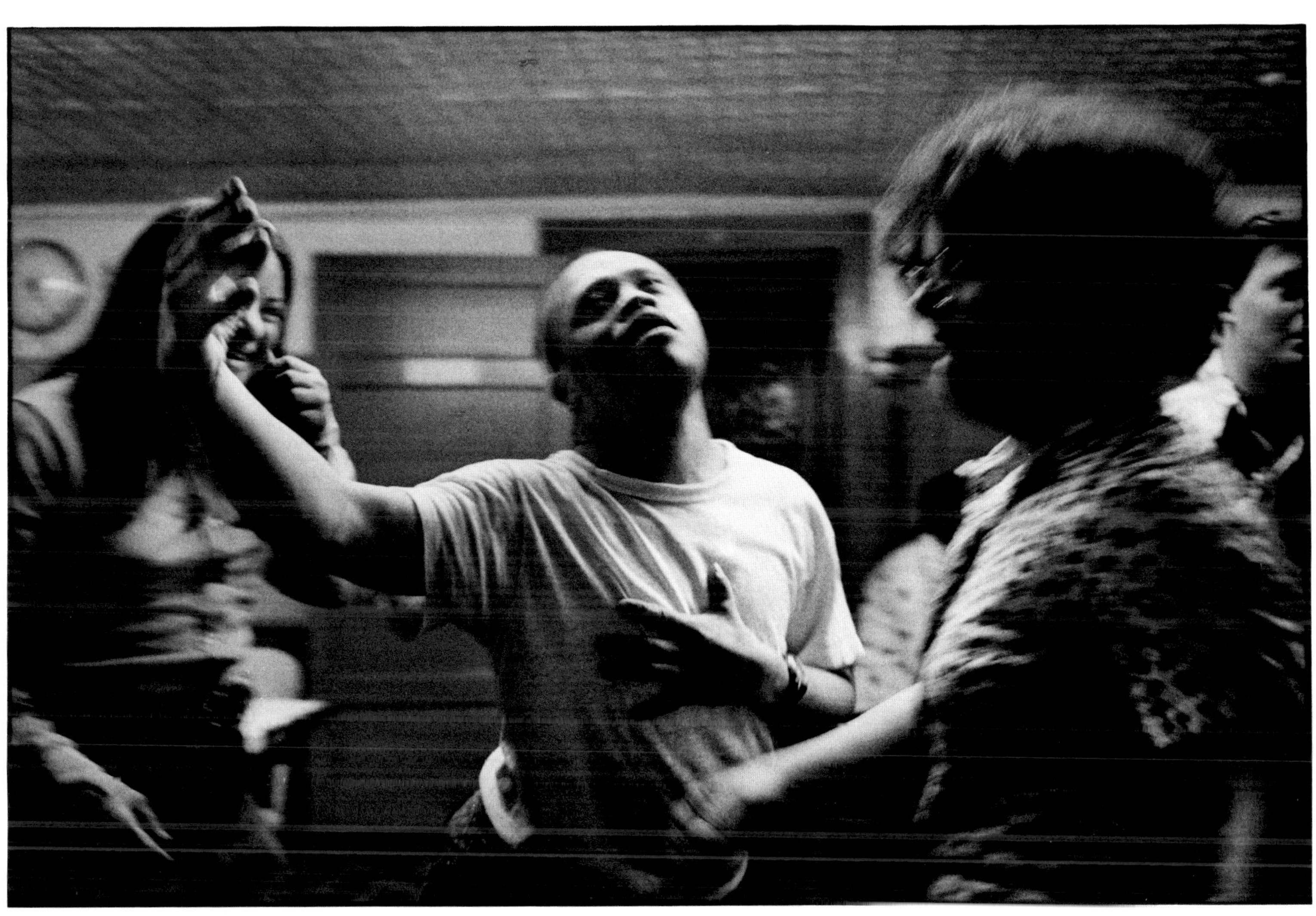

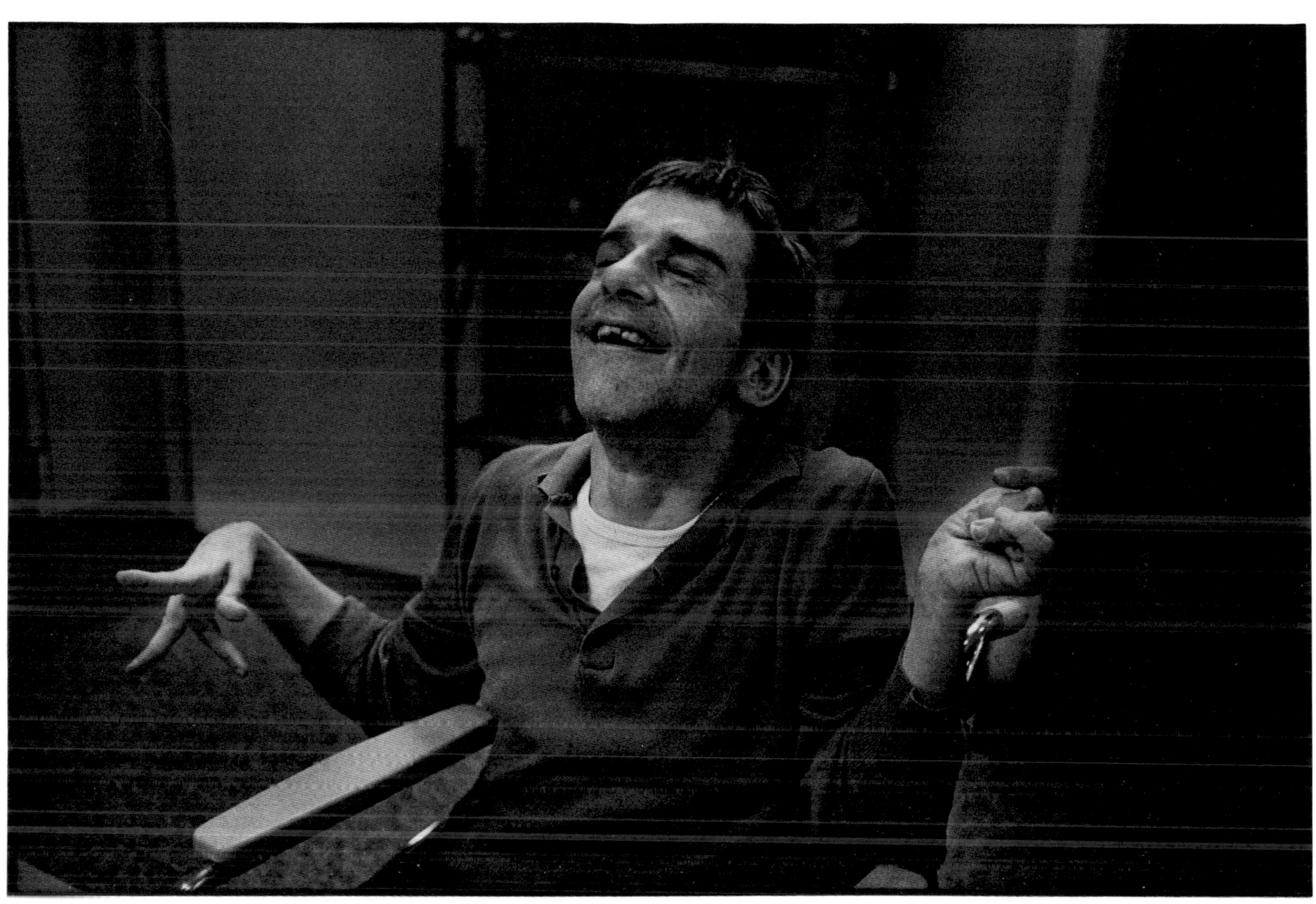

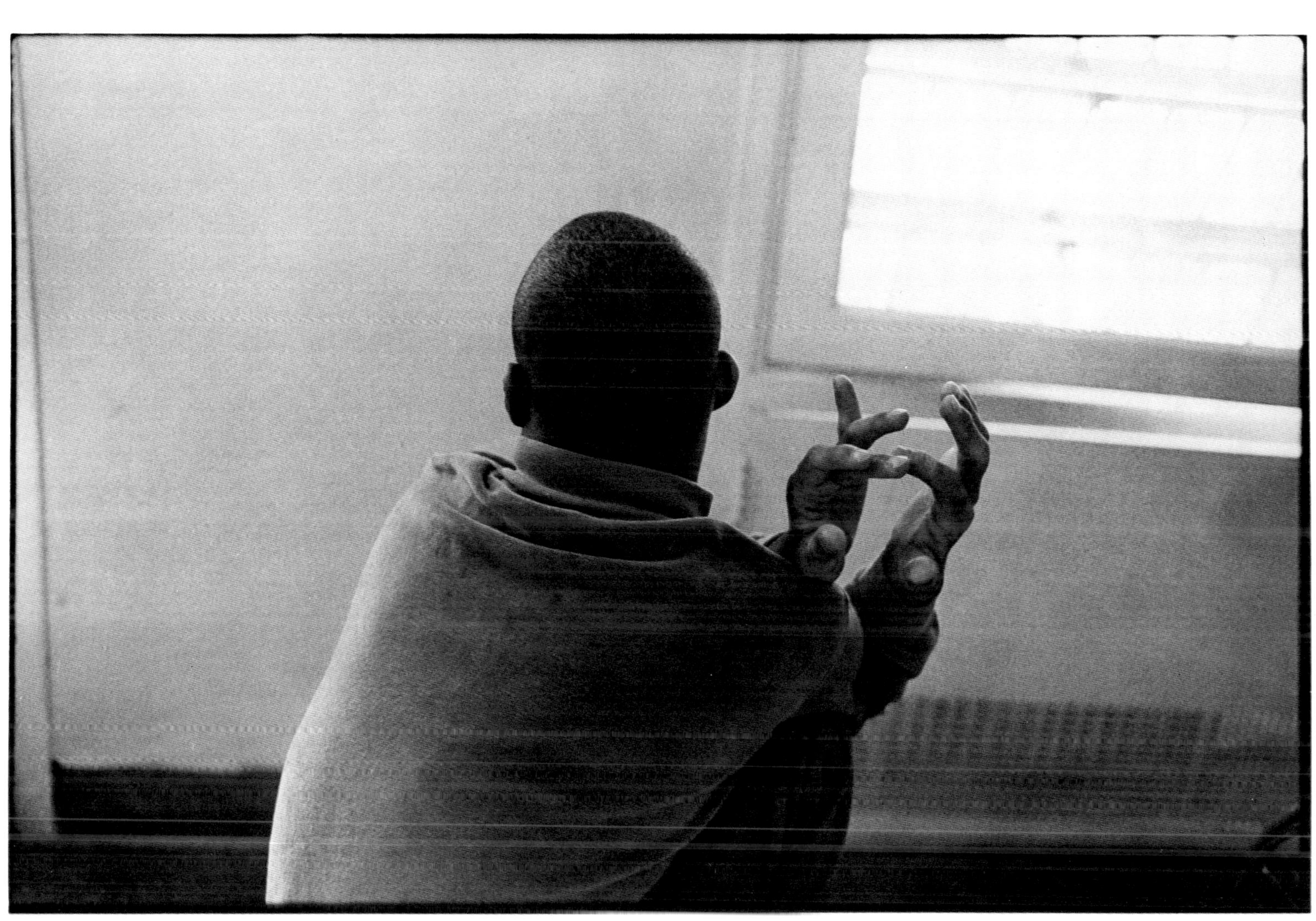

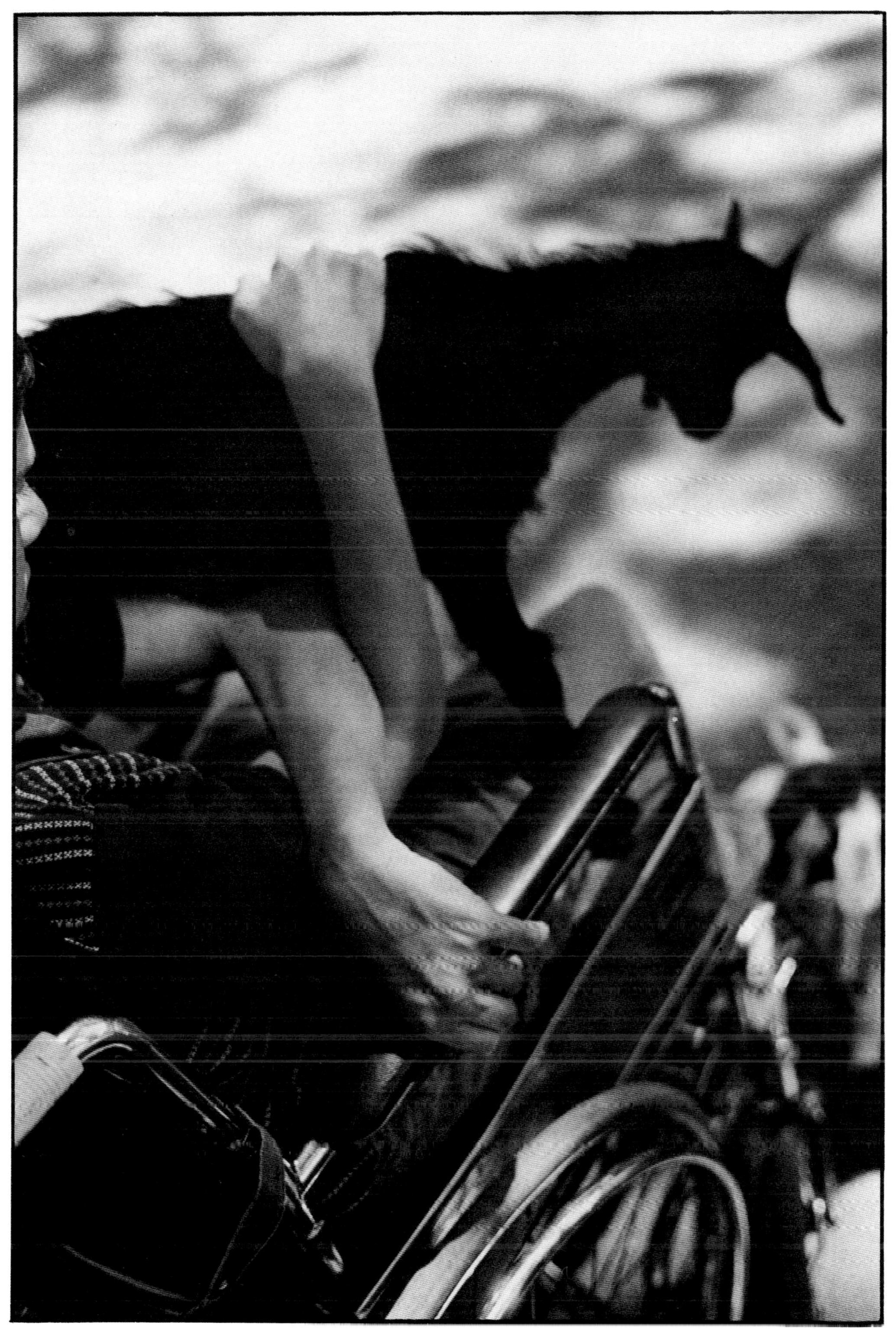

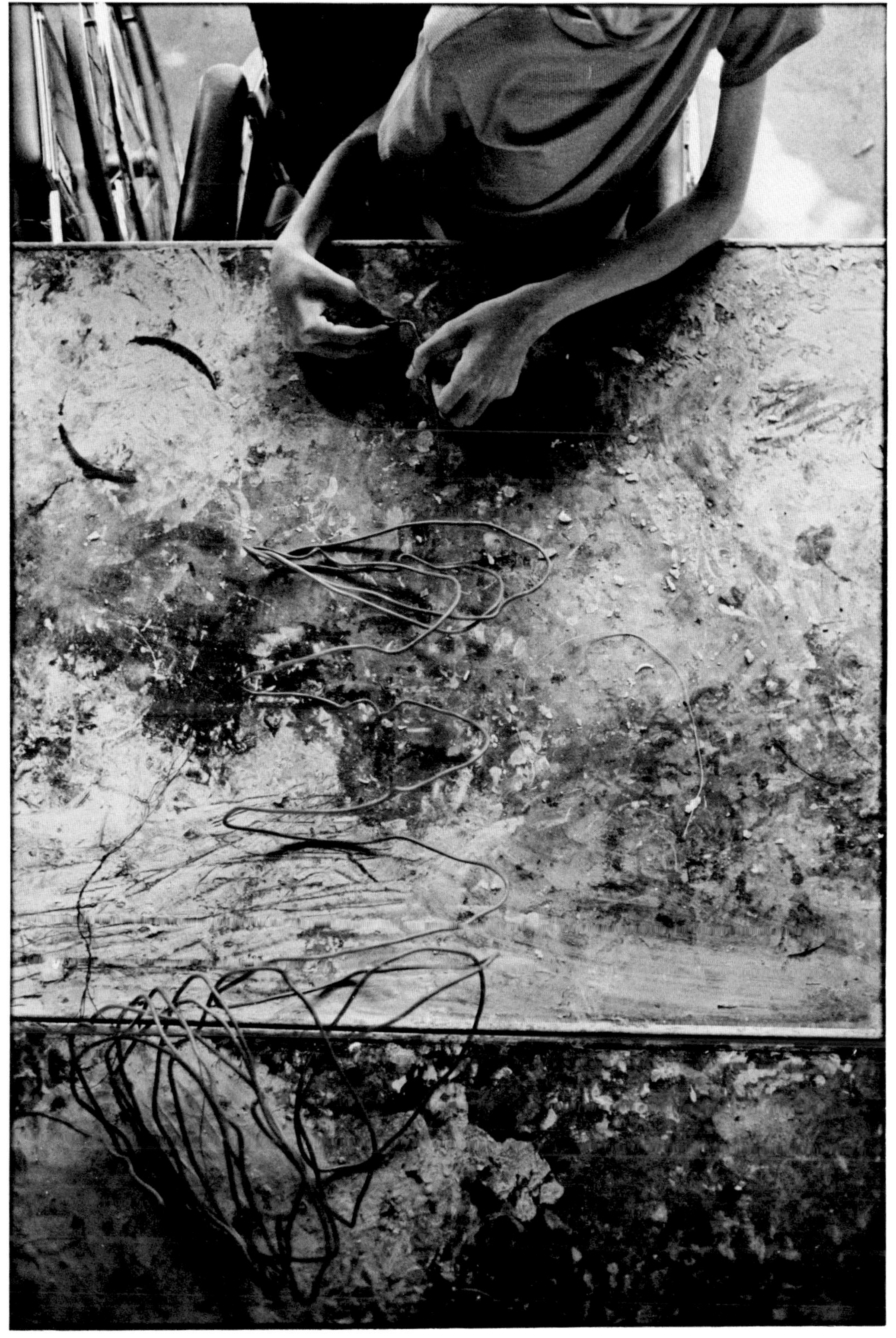

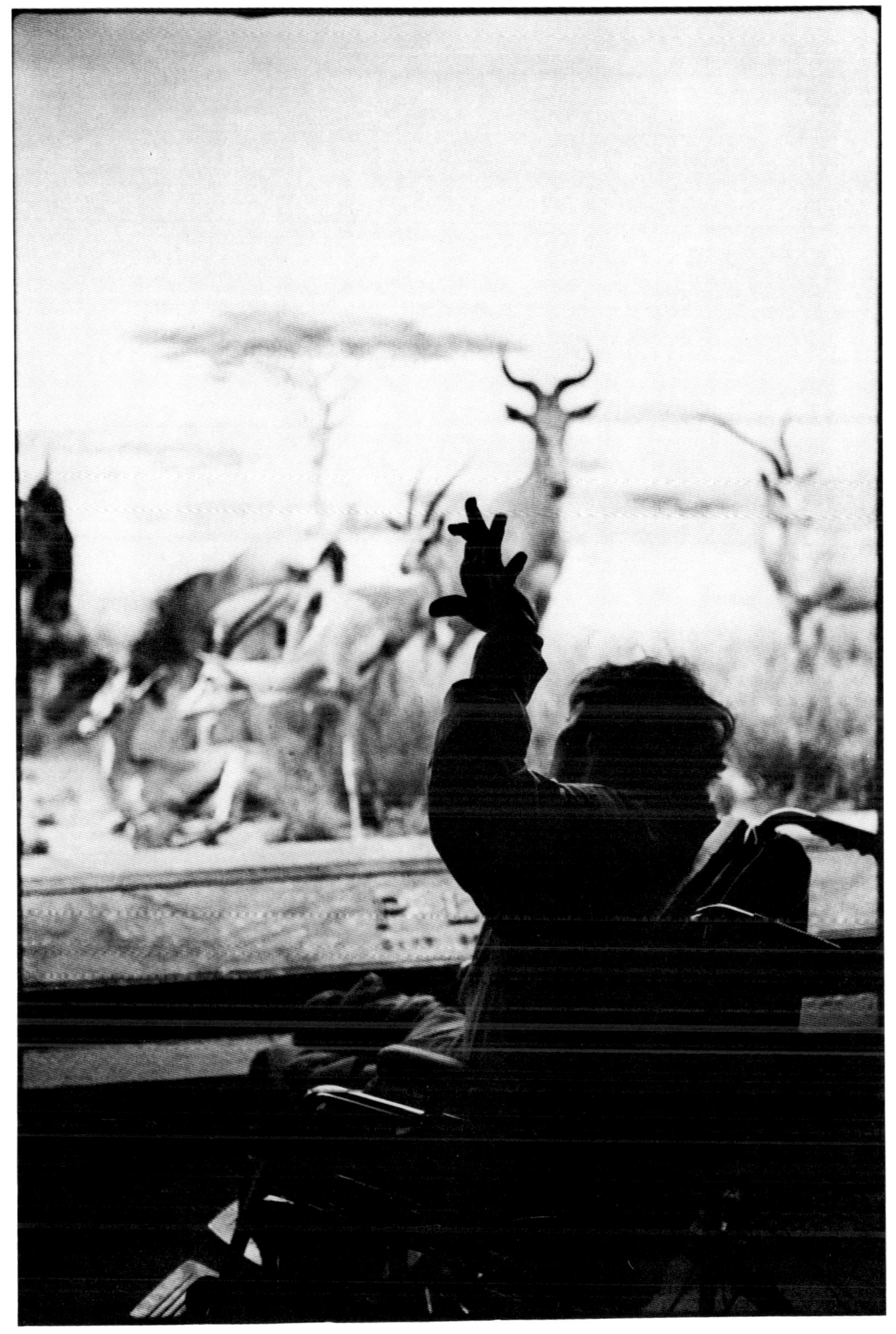

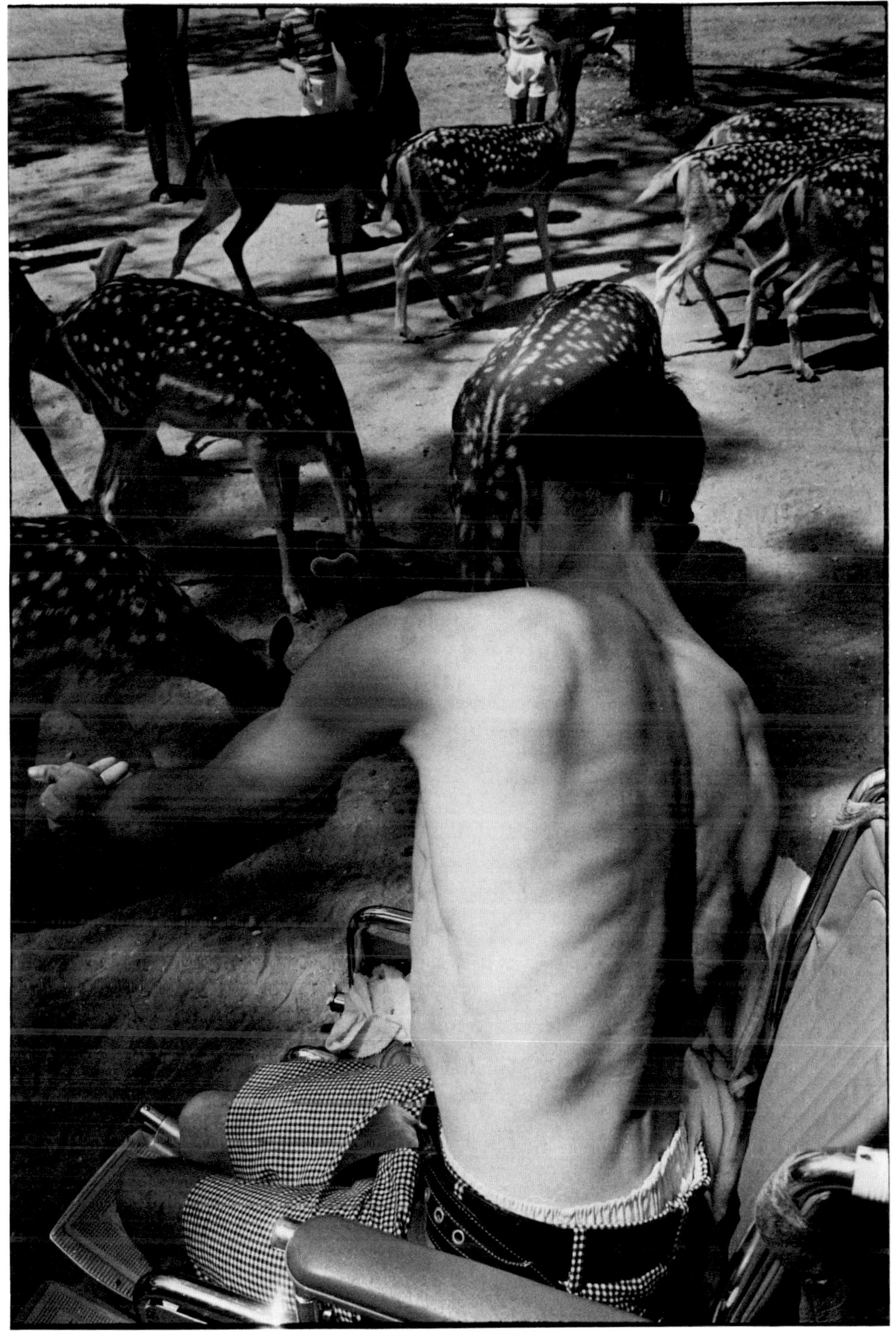

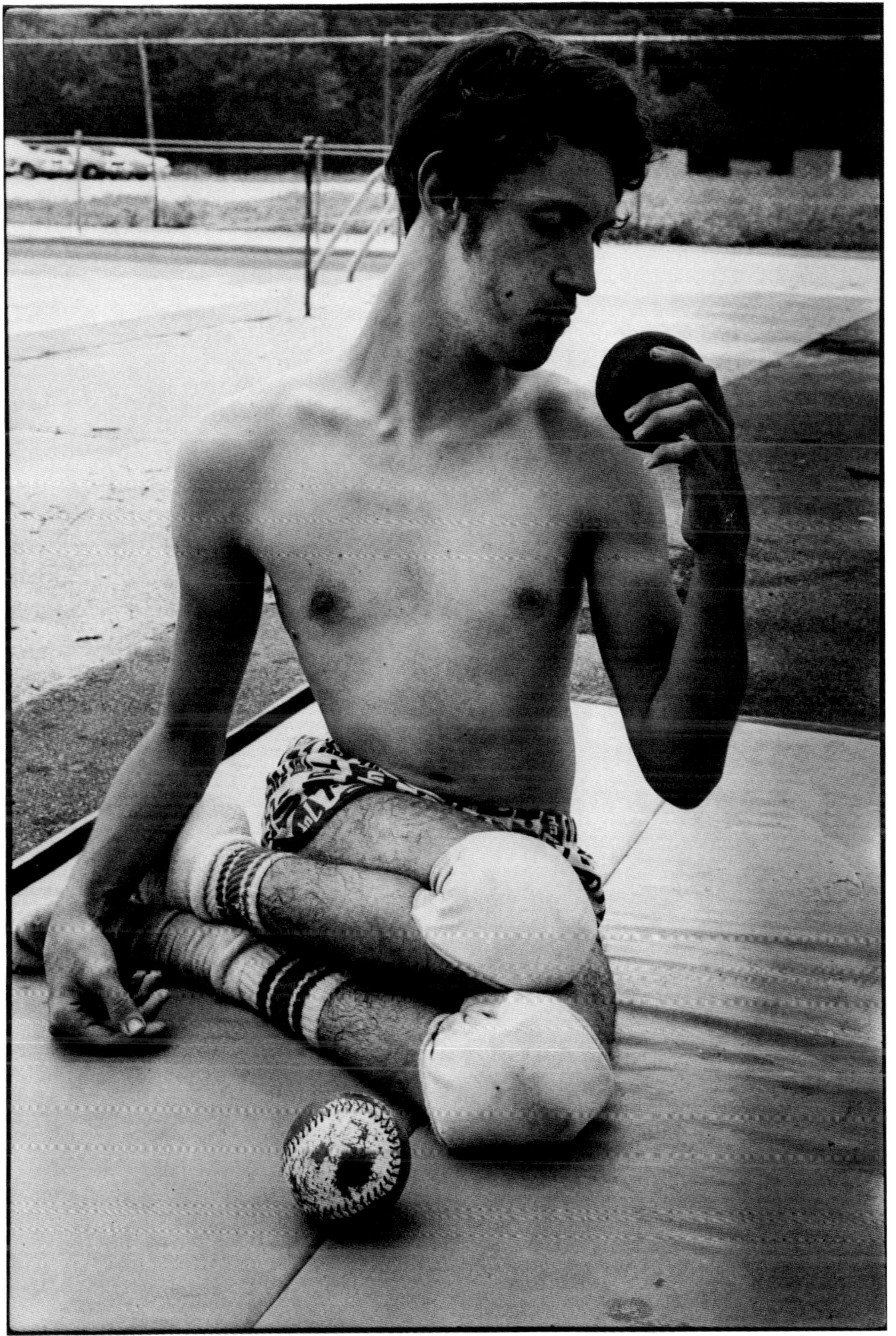

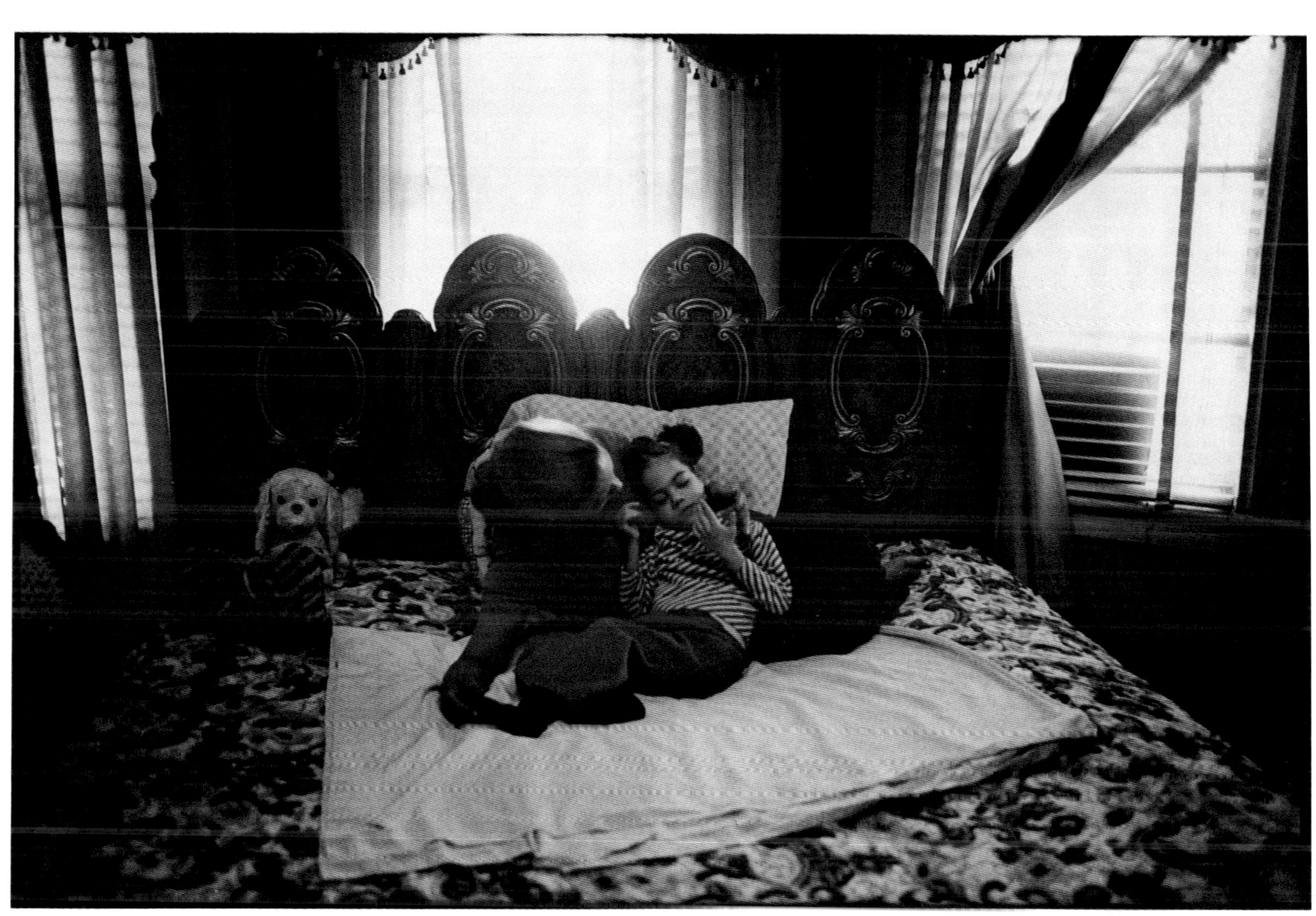

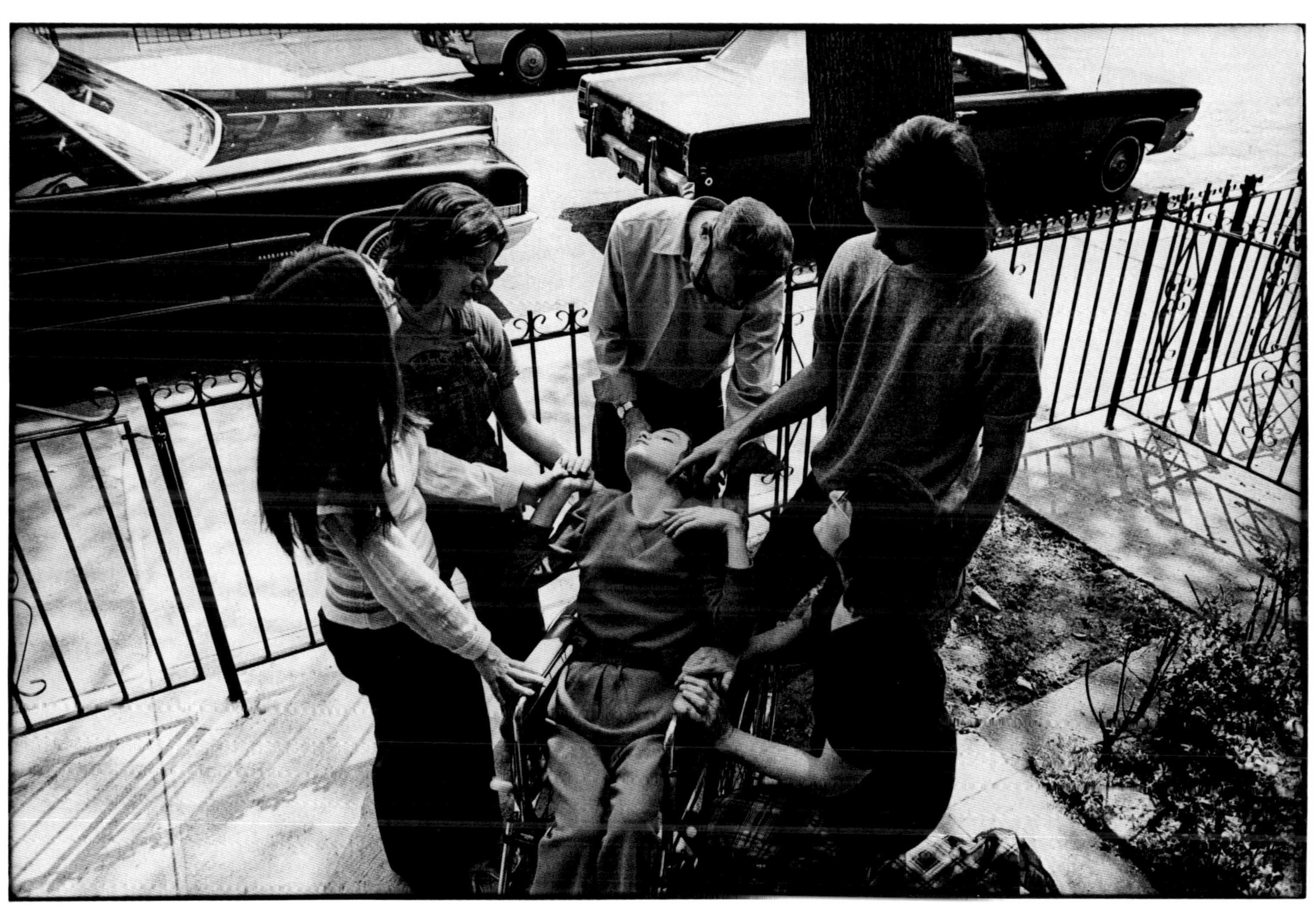

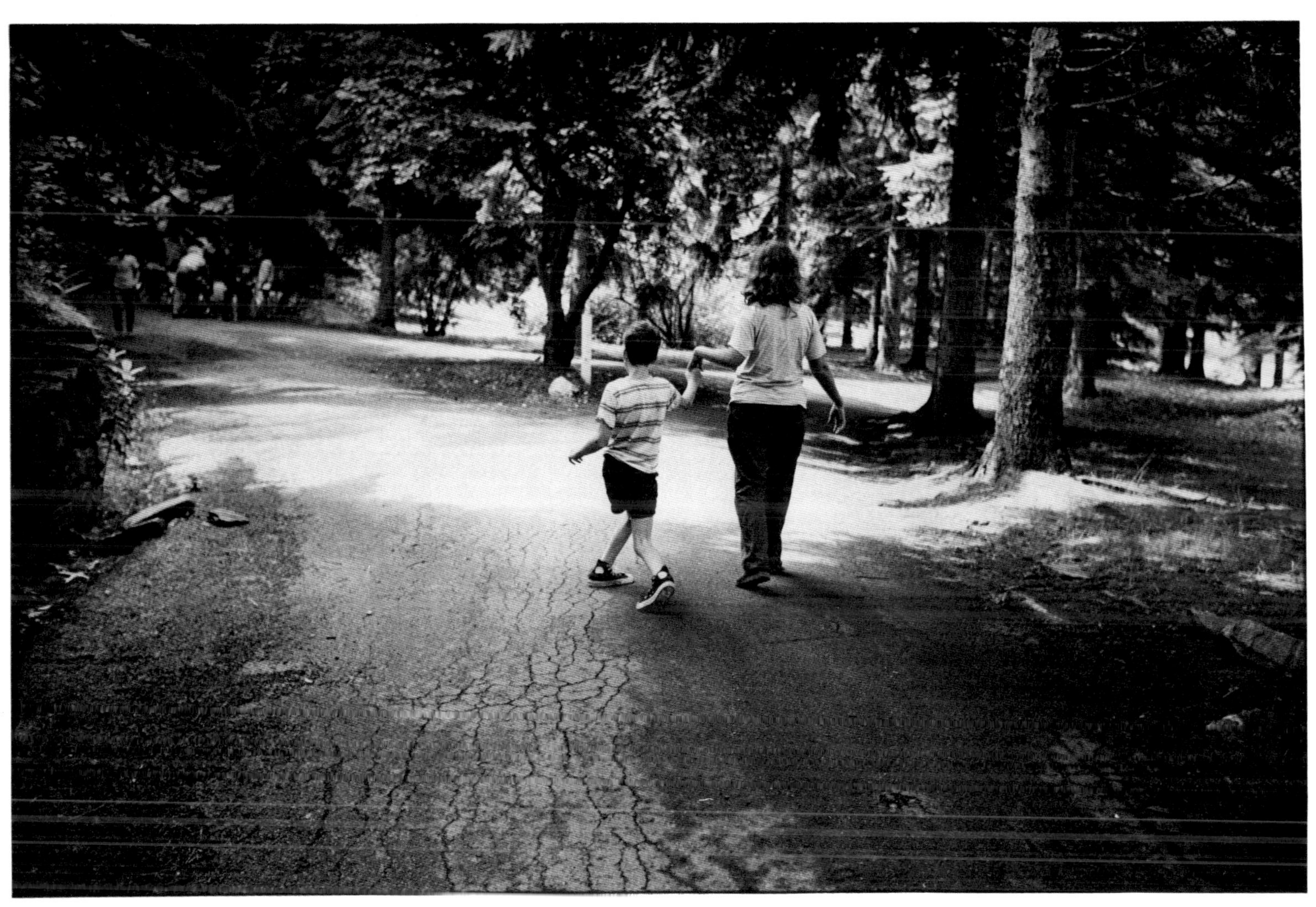

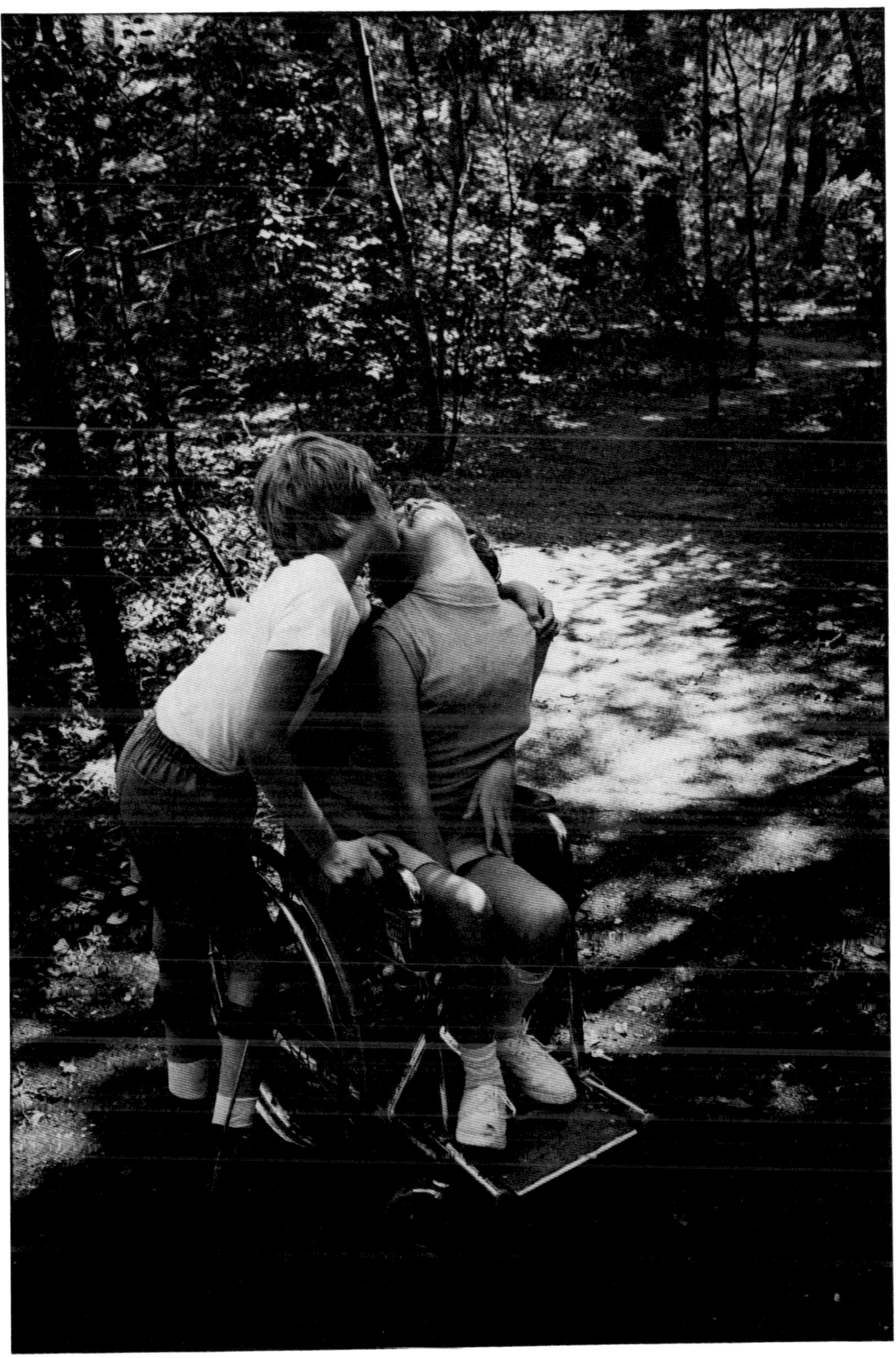

ACKNOWLEDGMENTS

I would like to thank all the people who made this book possible:

The administrators and staff of the places where the photographs were taken: Mr. Jacob Igra of the Jerusalem Institute for the Blind; Mr. Zev Weiss, Dr. Jack Gorelick, and Regina Schattner of the Association for the Help of Retarded Children; Dr. Bernard Tesse, Mr. Bert Piltz, Dr. Camilla Jones, Mr. Joseph Sardi, Sandra Gorenstein, Mr. Eddie Moore, Mrs. Mildred Adler, Rabbi Charles Hoffman, Anne Bettman, Bruce Donatuti, Jeff Seibel, Ellie Cohen, Henry Geller, Joan Sherman, Dianne Duggan, Pam Shoemaker, and Dvorah Kreppar of the Bernard Fineson Developmental Center. The families who let me come into their homes: Mrs. Elba Renta and her daughter Janette, Mr. and Mrs. Fitzpatrick and their daughter Tara, Mr. and Mrs. Fitzsimmons and their child Suzanne, Mrs. Ruth Jackson and her son Artis, Mr. and Mrs. Feely and their daughter Catherine, Mrs. Mary Burk and her daughter Nancy, Mr. and Mrs. Hughes and their son Scott, Mrs. Dockery and her daughter Margaret, Mrs. Shadiak and her daughter Renée, Mrs. Morrison and her daughter Frances, Mrs. Mary Cummings and her daughter Dorothy. Dr. Owen Bernstein, Mr. Thomas Shirtz, Mr. Lou Chaiken, Mr. Sam Wilson, Father Cribbins, Rabbi Wullinger, Nona Koch, and Marsha Perlmutter of the Brooklyn Developmental Center. Mr. Salvatore Gullo, Monica Willoughby Grey, Marilyn Orgel, and Mr. Norman Kimball of the United Cerebral Palsy Association. Mary Jane O'Neill, Harlan Conti, George Bennette, Kenneth Phillips, and Simone Rollins of the New York Association for the Blind. The directors of the summer camps I visited: William Brown and Richard Steinberg of Wagon Road Camp; Sheldon Koy and David Arnou of Camp Jened; Miss Marie Olson of Camp Hope; Michael Larsen and Iran Buckler of Camp Catskill; Michael Seeliger of Camp Cummings; Leroy Reynolds and Jim Flanigan of the Special Olympics. Lorraine Kisly, Susan Bergholz, Karen Chao, and Barbara Gutoff, the staff of *Parabola* magazine. My special editor at Knopf, Toinette Lippe. And last, my wife, Dvorah, for her unfailing support and faith.

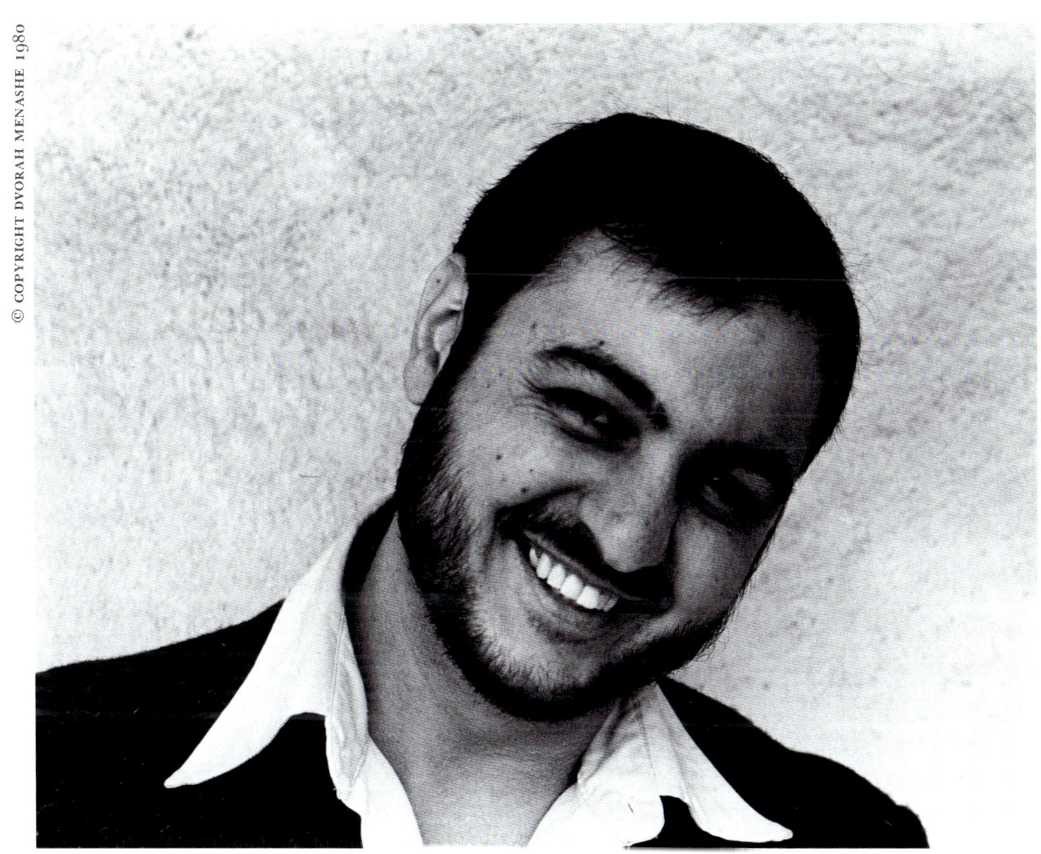

Born in Egypt in 1951, Abraham Menashe is a freelance photographer living in New York City. He is self-taught and is committed to photography that inspires, uplifts, and offers a healing vision. His work is in the archives of the Museum of Modern Art, the Metropolitan Museum of Art, and the Jewish Museum

A Note on the Book

Most of the photographs in this book were taken at residential state institutions, summer camps, and private family homes in New York City and Long Island. All are candid and uncropped, and made in available light with a 35-mm camera.

The book is published in conjunction with an exhibition at the Witkin Gallery, New York City, January 23–March 1, 1980.

The text of this book was set on the Linotype in a type face called Baskerville. The face is a facsimile reproduction of types cast from molds made for John Baskerville (1706–1775) from his designs. The punches for the revived Linotype Baskerville were cut under the supervision of the English printer George W. Jones. John Baskerville's original face was one of the forerunners of the type style known as "modern face" to printers.

Composed by Haber Typographers Inc., New York City.
Printed by the Morgan Press Inc., Dobbs Ferry, N.Y.,
on Warren's Lustro Offset Enamel Dull White 80 lb. paper
supplied by the Lindenmeyr Paper Corporation, Long Island City, N.Y.
Bound by American Book-Stratford Press Inc., Saddle Brook, N.J.
Designed by Judith Henry.